THE WISDOM
OF THE
SOLOMONS

by Elspeth McFadden

AmErica House
Baltimore

First printing

Biblical references are taken from the NIV.

ISBN: 1-58851-596-6
PUBLISHED BY AMERICA HOUSE BOOK
PUBLISHERS
www.publishamerica.com
Baltimore

Printed in the United States of America

To my son Toby,

my first and best editor

PETER'S STORY
(Proverbs 14: 21, 30, 31)

It was a frosty Saturday in February and the Solomons' back yard was piled high with packing snow. That could mean only one thing to seven-year-old Peter Solomon: he had to build a snow fort. He called for his friend, Bobby Pastorelli, and the two of them spent most of the morning creating two high barriers that could be used for battles between them.

The boys then collected the snow that remained and were busily forming snowballs of various sizes for their arsenals, when Peter stumbled upon it. Over by the garden shed, right up against the back fence, lay an animal.

"Bobby, Bobby, come here!" Peter called.

"No way, man. You just want to pelt me with snowballs from close up!"

"No, Bobby, you have to come. It's an animal, and I think it's sick or something."

Neither Peter nor Bobby recognized the animal, because it was so small and it was so tightly curled up. Its fur was grayish brown with black markings. It was trembling. From the cold or from sickness or from fear, Peter and Bobby didn't know.

"We should call your mom, don't you think?" Bobby suggested.

"I don't know. She doesn't like to be disturbed when she's working on a project. But this is important, isn't it?" Peter didn't want to leave the little creature, and he knew he had to be heard in his mom's upstairs studio, so he bellowed, "MOMMY!!!"

Bobby winced from Peter yelling in his ear. Both boys turned and looked up, and there was Peter's mother, Julianna

Solomon, scowling as she peered out an upper story window.

Peter's mom took only a moment to survey the scene below her window and decide that she needed to investigate. She disappeared from the window and reappeared in a few moments at the back door, snow boots on and winter coat slung over her shoulders.

"What's this all about, Peter?" she asked crisply as she strode across the back yard, putting her coat on properly against the cold. "What are you looking at?"

"It's some kind of animal, Mommy, and it looks sick." He moved to give his mom room to look closely at the helpless creature, whose breathing seemed raspy but regular in spite of its shivering.

"Oh, my goodness," Julianna said when she had had a good look. "It's a baby raccoon. I wonder what it's doing around here without its mother. Poor little thing."

"Can we keep it, Mommy?" Peter begged. "Somebody needs to make it healthy. I could do that. Pleeease."

"I'd help too, Mrs. Solomon," Bobby chimed in.

"Well, it isn't that simple with raccoons, boys. Raccoons aren't pets, they're wild animals. They are meant to live in the open, not in a cage or inside a house. We'll have to call someone for advice. We don't want the little guy to die, do we?" Julianna took one last look at the struggling creature and headed back to the house. "You stay out here and keep an eye on him while I make some calls. But don't pet him and don't get too close. If he's sick, it could be rabies, and trust me, you don't want to get rabies. Is that clear, boys?"

Both boys nodded sincerely, and then turned back to their patient.

After watching silently for a few minutes, Peter leaned over and reached out his hand.

"No!" Bobby exclaimed, catching Peter's arm and pulling it back. "You heard what your mom said: no touching!"

"But he looks so sad and so cold. I can hardly stand to see him this way. I just wanted to make him feel better."

"Yeah, me too. But we can't. Not till we find out if he has rabies or something like that. Your mom made it sound really dangerous."

"He doesn't look dangerous, though, does he? He just looks afraid and sick. What can we do for him?"

"Your mom said no touching. We could pray for him, though. God loves animals too, you know."

"We'll need a name then, won't we? Just in case God's not sure which raccoon we're talking about."

"Oh, Peter, he knows. But let's give him a name anyway. What d'you think?"

"Anything but Rocky. All racoons get called Rocky."

"How about Ricky, then?"

Peter laughed. "Yeah, that's good. Ricky. How are you doing there, little Ricky Raccoon? We're here to watch over you, and now we're going to ask God to watch over you too. He's the Big Guy. He'll get you healthy. Okay, Bobby, you pray and I'll pray, and Ricky will be fine." Peter and Bobby bowed their heads over the trembling baby raccoon, and sent the "desires of their hearts" to God.

It wasn't long until the back door swung open, and Julianna came outside again, followed by a small red-haired man in a navy blue uniform. The badge on his coat read "Society for Animal Protection", and he was carrying a small cage.

"Oh no, Mommy, you're not going to let this man take Ricky away, are you?" Peter begged.

"Yes, Peter, that's exactly what is going to happen," Julianna said firmly. "This is Mr. DelSorto, and he is going to take good care of him."

Mr. DelSorto held out his hand to shake Peter's hand and then Bobby's. Peter felt better when he had felt Mr. DelSorto's firm handshake and looked into his kind eyes. Perhaps it would be alright for Ricky after all.

"Here's what we're going to do for Ricky," the uniformed man explained. "First of all, we'll take him to the animal doctor and see why he's shivering and wrapped up like that. She may be able to figure out why Ricky's on his own without his mother. He'll have to be checked for disease he can spread to humans, too, of course. Later, when he's healthy, we'll take him outside the city to a place where other raccoons live."

"He looks pretty sick," Peter said. "What if he doesn't get better? What will happen to him then?"

"That's a good question, Peter. If he doesn't get healthy enough to make it on his own, we have a few animal shelters and zoos that take our animals and make their lives as healthy as possible. How does that sound?"

Peter looked down at Ricky, whose big black eyes were now open and looking straight at Peter. Peter's heart was sore.

"I guess that'll be alright. It's the best we can do for him, right, Mom?"

"Yes, honey, it is."

Mr. DelSorto put on some heavy gloves before he bent down and gently lifted Ricky into the cage, which Peter noticed contained a towel on the bottom and some food. Mr. DelSorto spoke quietly to Ricky all the time he was handling him. You could tell he loved animals.

When Mr. DelSorto left carrying the cage, the yard seemed suddenly empty, but Peter knew they had done the best they could for Ricky Raccoon.

* * *

The next Saturday, very early in the morning, Peter raced into the family room and was about to launch himself into his favorite TV watching chair when he noticed that his father,

Jake Solomon, was already in it, sipping his morning coffee. Before he landed with a crash in his dad's lap, Peter veered to the right a bit and landed instead on the big ottoman in front of the chair.

"Hey, Dad," he yelped in surprise, "what are you doing up?"

Peter's clock had read 6 - 2 - 4. Peter thought he would have the house to himself for a while.

"Hey, Pete," his dad replied, chuckling, "I could ask you the same thing."

"I'm always up early Saturdays. It's my cartoon day."

"Oh, yeah? Well, I woke up early this morning and I couldn't get back to sleep. So is it okay with you if I just sit with you for a bit?"

Peter was looking around frantically for the TV remote, when he noticed that his father had something in his hand. It was a paper. Looking closer, he saw that it was a story he had written at school. His first grade teacher, Mrs. Dunn, had assigned them the topic "My Family", and after they had written about the people in their family they drew pictures of themselves and their family for a bulletin board display. Mrs. Dunn had really liked his drawing. She had liked his story too, even though she thought he had used the word "nice" too often. Peter didn't like the story very much, though.

"That's my story," Peter said, reaching over to snatch it from Jake.

"Yes," his father said, "I found it on the kitchen table. I was just going to read it, but now that you're here – and since you grabbed it from me – would you read it for me?"

Peter wrinkled his nose. He wanted to watch TV, not read his dumb story. It was hard for him to sit still and slowly read the story aloud.

My Family, by Peter Solomon
I have a nice family. My mom and my dad are nice. My

big brother, Tim, is nice and he plays baseball. My big sister, Taylor, is nice, and she has lots of friends. My other big sister, Emma, is sometimes nice and she plays the violin. Then there is me.

Jake smiled when he was finished. "Great story, Pete," he said. But then, parents always liked what their kids did, didn't they? "So I'm nice, am I? I hope you'll remember that the next time I have to send you to your room." Jake winked at his younger son. "You know what, though? You said something special about all the kids in the family except yourself."

"Oh, did I?"

"Yes, you did. You mentioned Tim's baseball, Taylor's social life, and Emma's music. All true, but what about you, Pete? How are you special?"

Peter had rolled the story into a tube. His hands wouldn't keep still. "Ah, Dad... Can we watch TV now? I usually watch Blue Bird and the Gang at 6 - 3 - 0."

Jake nodded and patted the space beside him in the big chair. Peter happily snuggled in beside him to watch the program.

Blue Bird and the gang turned out to be a rerun, about the time the gang were taking part in a baseball tournament. Blue Bird was pitcher, of course, because he was the leader of the gang; but Snaggleduff wanted to pitch as well...

Then Peter was remembering a day last summer when he and his brother Tim, who was twelve, were playing catch in the backyard. Peter always liked playing ball with his big brother. Tim played on two baseball teams, one for the town and one for the school, so he could teach Peter a lot. That day they were trying to strengthen their arms, and they were also working on accuracy in their pitches.

Everything was fine until Tim's best friend, Ryan Barnicke, arrived with Buzz Baxter, one of their teammates on the

Parkesville Panthers. Ryan and Buzz had joined in their practice, but it wasn't long until Peter had left in tears. Peter just couldn't reach some of the balls that came his way, because he was short, even for a seven-year-old. Then Ryan had thrown a ball so hard that his hand really hurt, even though he had caught it just right.

As Peter sat half-listening to Blue Bird and the gang, he could remember the feeling – pain in his hand and arm and pain in his heart. *I'll never catch up to those guys. I'll never be as good as them! Even if I grow, I'll never be any good!* He remembered Tim calling after him to come back, but he had just gone to his room to play with his action figures. He could still hear Tim's voice yelling, "C'mon, Peter. You'll be able to handle those before you know it!" Yeah, right.

Peter's attention was suddenly drawn to a commercial for Lettuce Leaf dolls, the latest toy sensation for girls. One of the girls on the ad had a Lettuce Leaf doll in her arms, and of course she was surrounded by a crowd of admiring girls and boys. *Man, she's just like Taylor. Everyone wants to be her friend...*

Tim's twin sister, Taylor, was in many ways Tim's opposite. For one thing, he was a boy and she was a girl! Also, where Tim took everything seriously and followed every rule, Taylor turned everything into fun and bent the rules now and then. The only thing she shared with Tim, besides blond hair, was a love of sports. Like Tim, Taylor played on just about every sports team available for her age group. She could run fast, get lots of baskets, score goals, whatever the sport called for. But what made Taylor a standout in Peter's mind was her team spirit. Taylor could get along with *anyone.*

For Peter, Taylor's team spirit translated into a steady stream of 7th grade girls in and out of the Solomon home. They would be laughing and giggling and talking about things that Peter didn't understand. Sometimes they would even look at him and say something and then laugh and giggle. He really hated that. Other times, they'd come in and ruffle his hair. He hated that even more!

But what Peter hated most was how lonely it made him feel to see all those friends that Taylor had collected. Peter himself found it hard to make friends. Bobby Pastorelli lived right next door and came over often to play, but when the house was full of Taylor's friends and he was playing all alone, it was hard. *I'll never be as popular as Taylor,* Peter would sometimes think to himself. *Nobody likes me.*

"So what do we watch at 7 - 0 - 0?" Peter's daydream was interrupted by his dad's question. Blue Bird and the gang was over already. Peter had missed the ending. He hoped Snaggleduff's baseball experiences were made happier by all the friends he had in the gang.

"There's either Aladdin or Matt's Rats. Do you care which one we watch?"

"Well, I'd choose Aladdin, if it was only me."

"Oh, okay." Peter was hoping for Matt's Rats, but he took the controller and found the channel for Aladdin.

Aladdin and Jasmine were wandering the streets of Agrabah on market day when they came upon a snake charmer. He was playing his flute, and the charmed snake was dancing out of the woven basket. Suddenly a chase was on, and Aladdin picked up Jasmine and climbed the back of the startled snake to escape the soldiers who were chasing him...

Aladdin's adventure with the snake charmer made Peter think about Emma, who was nine years old. Everyone always raved about what a talented musician she was. She could probably charm snakes with her violin. What people didn't know about her was that she also had a talent for tormenting her younger brother. No one knew how mean Emma could be, because to everyone else she appeared to be quiet and shy. Little did they know.

If Peter was drawing, Emma would walk by and whisper, "What's that you're drawing, a mess in a barnyard?"

If Peter was shooting baskets, Emma would run by, steal the ball, and throw it away into the bushes. "Oh, sorry, Peter," she would chant as she ran off.

If Peter was working on his homework, Emma would look down at his work and say, "Come on, Peter, anybody knows that's the wrong answer. How'd you get to be so dumb?"

If Peter was walking home from school with Bobby, Emma would race by with her friends, saying, "Hi Bobby." To Peter, she would say nothing.

Sometimes Peter would stop and listen to Emma as she practiced her violin. He had to admit she was pretty good, even if it wasn't his favorite kind of music. But if Emma caught him standing there, she'd say, "Go away, Petey. I can't concentrate when you're staring at me like that!"

Peter didn't know why Emma always had to be so mean to him, but these days he found it best to avoid her altogether. In fact, he was pretty much avoiding all his siblings. He just wasn't in their league.

Again, he was startled back to "the real world" by his dad's voice. "Hey Pete, you're certainly far away. What are you thinking about?"

"Oh, I don't know."

"Come on, bud. You seem upset, and you haven't really been your cheerful self lately. What's up?" Jake gave his son's shoulder a squeeze of encouragement and turned off the TV.

Peter was surprised by the words that flew out of his mouth. "I'm tired of being the youngest in the family."

"Tired of being the youngest? Your brother and sisters picking on you?"

Peter thought about Emma, but decided not to rat on his sister. Not yet, anyway. "No. I was just thinking about the twins and Emma and about how much better they are than me."

"Better?"

"Yeah. They can do everything so much better than me. They're all amazing, and I'm not."

"Oh Peter, I'm so sorry you feel that way. Because you're amazing, too, you know."

"No, I'm not. I'm short, I'm dumb, I can't catch a ball, I'm no good at music. I'm just me, nothing special at all."

"That's where you're wrong." Jake reached for Peter to slide him over onto his lap. "Listen, you're right that you're not like the other three. Your mom and I are always marveling at how different our children are from each other. It's part of the amazing way God has put the world together. Everyone has special talents that God gives them, which he wants us to use for his work here on earth. We call them gifts. Your gifts are different from everyone else's gifts. If they weren't, it would be a pretty boring old life, wouldn't it?"

"Talents. I don't have any talents. Everyone is better than me at everything." Peter was staring at his hands, which were still busy unrolling and re-rolling his story paper.

"Now Peter, that's just not true. Remember when the Pastorellis moved here all the way from Florida. Bobby was really shy and hardly ever came out of the house. Well, you went in after him. You knew he was hurting and you worked hard to get him out of his shell. Now, of course, you two are best buds. But lots of other kids would have decided he was 'weird' and just left him alone. You saw that his feelings were hurt and you helped him. You don't think that's a talent?"

"Well, maybe..." Peter mumbled. "I just knew he had to come out and play and he'd feel better."

"Then there's Mrs. Worthington," his dad continued. "Ever since Mr. Worthington died last month, you've been going over to visit with Mrs. Worthington whenever you get a chance."

"I don't want her to be lonely, all by herself in that big house."

"And I'm so proud of the way you have reached out to her. I know you put a smile on her face whenever you're there."

Peter was still playing with the rolled-up story in his hands, his head bowed. "So what's special about that? That's just what I do. I don't score goals, and memorize music for recitals, and impress lots of people."

"Well, you impress me, bud. Still not convinced? Okay, think back to last week and Ricky Raccoon. Do you think your brother would have cared about a sick raccoon the way you did? I don't think so. He would have alerted your mother and gone on with his business, not thinking too much about it. Wouldn't he?"

"Yeah, probably."

"And how would the girls have reacted, do you think?"

It was funny to imagine Taylor's reaction. Peter was smiling up at his dad, through shaggy bangs, when he said, "Taylor would have screamed and jumped up and down, probably, until the whole neighborhood was in the yard!"

Jake laughed. "And poor little Ricky would have been paralyzed with fright! And what about Emma?"

"She never goes outside at all, if she can help it."

"So, you see, Peter, you accepted responsibility for that raccoon's situation in a way your siblings would not have. That's your gift, Peter – caring about others, people and animals. I have no doubt in my mind, Peter, that God is smiling as he watches you grow, because you care about his creations. You know how your mom and I love the Proverbs. I've got a couple of proverbs for you, Peter. 'Blessed is he who is kind to the needy' – that's you, Pete. Also, "Whoever is kind to the needy honors God." And, Pete, do you know what envy is?"

"Yeah. It's when you want something someone else has."

"Like wishing you were just like your big brother, or had the same abilities as your sisters, right? Well, here's a proverb to warn you: "envy rots the bones." I just love that one; the way

15

Solomon expresses the power of envy to mess us up. What could be worse than having your bones rot? That's how powerful envy can be if it takes root in us. A big lesson for a little guy. Are you up to it?"

"I'll try, Dad."

"Now, do you think I've lectured you long enough?" Peter nodded sheepishly up at his dad. "Okay, then, I've got some news for you. Mr. DelSorto called yesterday to tell you that Ricky is doing very nicely at the shelter and he wondered if you wanted to go and visit before they release him back into the wild. What do you think, Pete?"

"Cool! Can we go today, Dad?"

"I thought you might say that! I don't see why not! But first, how would you feel about a big serving of Papa's Pack-a-Punch Pancakes?" Peter grinned and gave Jake a quick hug, before he slid down from his dad's lap and led the way to the kitchen.

By the time the other members of the Solomon family staggered sleepily into the kitchen, lured there by the delicious aroma of Jake's cooking, father and son were enjoying a pancake feast and celebrating the wisdom of a young Solomon, who was learning to appreciate his own gifts and the gifts of others.

WHO'S THE BOSS?
(Daniel 6; Proverbs 10: 17, 16: 7, 15: 3;
Leviticus 19: 32; 1 Samuel 18-24)

Emma Solomon had some terrible news to share with her mother when she rushed through the kitchen door after school that Friday in March.

"Mrs. Harvey wasn't at school today, and we don't know when she'll be coming back," she said hesitantly.

"Oh, my goodness," said Julianna Solomon, "what's happened?" Julianna didn't expect much of an answer. Nine-year-old Emma was the shyest of the four Solomon children. The twelve-year-old twins, Tim and Taylor, had a lot more to say than she did, being so much older. Her younger brother, Peter, who was seven, spoke out whenever he felt like it. Emma sometimes wished she could be talkative like her siblings; but usually, at home, Emma kept things to herself.

Today, though, Emma wanted to talk.

"When the bell went this morning, Mrs. Harvey wasn't at the Junior door to bring us inside like she usually does. There was no teacher in our classroom either. Then Ms. Shaw came to our class, all out of breath. You could tell she was worried. Mrs. Harvey was in a car accident on the way to work. She had to go to the hospital. Isn't that horrible, Mommy?" Emma only called Julianna "Mommy" when she was really upset.

"The poor woman," Julianna sighed. Julianna was a big fan of Mrs. Harvey. She had taught both Tim and Taylor when they had been in fourth grade, and she had been the first teacher who seemed to value her twins as the very different individuals that they were. Emma adored her too, and was having her best year in school so far. Mrs. Harvey was one of those "old school"

17

teachers who managed to avoid all the trends that come and go in the education system; she just loved kids and taught them what they needed to know. But now she had been in an accident, and it seemed serious.

"So, who was your teacher today?"

"Ms. Shaw," Emma replied. "She's nice, but she said she has to go back to being Principal on Monday. I wonder who will come to teach us."

"Me, too. And we should pray for Mrs. Harvey's quick recovery," her mother added.

* * *

Parkesville is a small town, so the Solomons were able to find out through the grapevine on Saturday that Mrs. Harvey's injuries were, thankfully, not life-threatening. She had a few broken bones, and the doctors had had to operate to stop some internal bleeding. The good news was that she would be back, where she belonged, in her fourth grade classroom. The bad news was that no one was sure when.

And, for Emma, this was very bad news indeed.

* * *

The woman who met the Fourth Graders at the Junior door Monday morning was tall and very, very thin, so thin that Emma thought to herself, *She's all pointy!* She didn't seem to have a soft curve anywhere. She was dressed in black from her black button-down shirt and black jacket, down through her long straight black skirt, right to her sensible black shoes. She had tiny cold eyes behind black-rimmed glasses. She had a pinched look that made Emma think her face might crack if she smiled. Emma and her classmates looked up at her in stunned silence.

18

"Don't just stand there gawking, Fourth Graders," the "pointy lady" said sharply, "it's time to get to work. Let's go; no dawdling!" Emma thought she was going to say, "Spit spot!" next, like Mary Poppins. But no luck; she just gave them all a glare.

Emma caught the eyes of Rachel Cunningham. Rachel shared a table with Emma in Mrs. Harvey's class. "Yikes!' Rachel mouthed quietly and crossed her eyes. Emma couldn't help but giggle.

"What's so funny, young lady?" the "pointy lady" bellowed ferociously in Emma's direction.

Emma wanted to be able to crawl inside her jacket like a turtle into its shell – and never come out. She was horrified. All eyes were on her. She couldn't think of a thing to say. She couldn't even remember the question!

The "pointy lady" must have been able to read Emma's mind, because she repeated, "I said, 'What's so funny?' Don't just stare at me with your jaw hanging down to your chest!"

Suddenly Emma realized that her mouth was, in fact, hanging open. How embarrassing! Emma knew she was on the verge of tears, and she had to use all her energy not to cry.

"S... S... Sorry, ma'am. N... n... nothing, m... ma'am. P... P... Pardon?" Emma finally stammered.

Emma's attempts to answer went totally ignored. "Let's get a move on then. Everyone, into the classroom. Find your nametag and sit in that seat. Quickly, quickly. And no talking!"

Ms. Shaw, who was watching this scene from down the hall, had never seen the Fourth Grade class move so quickly or so quietly.

Inside the classroom, Emma and her friends were surprised to note that their familiar room had been totally rearranged. Gone was the Quiet Corner, where they could go when their work was done to read comfortably on pillows. Gone was the rocking chair where Mrs. Harvey would sit to tell them stories on Friday afternoons. If they were good, they could sometimes sit in this Special Chair to read their own stories to the class. Their tables, which they had shared with a partner, had been replaced by single desks, in rows facing the blackboard. Emma had to admit that it looked orderly, but it sure didn't look like fun.

Emma's heart sank even further when she finally found her nametag. Her desk was right at the back of the row nearest the windows. She didn't mind being near the windows, but her nearest neighbors, instead of her friend Rachel, were Donny Howard, who never did any work and was proud of this record, and Cathy Parker, who didn't behave very well and who had told everyone in the Fourth Grade that she didn't like Emma Solomon, "that goody-goody". And as if that wasn't bad enough, the desk of the "pointy lady" had been moved to the back of the room, right behind Emma's new seat.

Settling into her desk, Emma heard her new teacher say under her breath, "Oh, so her name is Emma..."

Oh help, Emma gasped.

* * *

Emma had never been so glad to get to the end of a school day. The only relief she had had from the pointy lady's staring eyes had been at morning recess and lunchtime, when she and her classmates had talked, comforting each other and trying to figure out what to do. But class time had been really painful! So when the bell rang, she pushed her way past Cathy and Donny in her rush to get to the hall, grab her coat, and leave the school. She had never felt this way before. She was mad, she was sad, and she wanted to say something really bad!

Julianna spotted her running up the sidewalk to their house, and she could see that her usually calm daughter was in tears. She hurried to meet her and hold her in a comforting hug.

"Emma, what's the matter?" It was a while before Emma could answer her through her sobs. Julianna knew she had to let her cry it out, but her daughter's sadness was painful to her while she waited.

When Emma could finally speak, her words came out in a flood. "She's so awful, Mommy. She picks on me, and she put me near Cathy and Donny, and I had to stay in for recess, and it wasn't my fault, and she moved our room all around, and we can't even say one word, and..."

"Slow down, my precious," Julianna said, soothingly. "Who are you talking about? Does this person have a name?"

"The new teacher, Miss Glass," Emma spat out. Julianna was shocked at the amount of anger and dislike that she heard in her daughter's voice.

"Oh honey, she's as terrible as all that?" Julianna asked gently.

"She hates me, Mommy. I didn't do anything. I just giggled at something Rachel did and she kept picking on me after that. And that was way long ago, this morning! I can't go back there!"

"Wait a minute, now, Em, let's talk about this a bit," Julianna said, going to the fridge. Emma settled herself at the breakfast bar. She needed both her hands to hold up her weary head. Julianna gently rubbed Emma's back after she joined her with juice and a snack for them to share. "Okay, now, details. Why can't you go back?"

"She's so mean. And she can't teach either. I don't know why they picked her! I'm not going back until Mrs. Harvey does!"

"Listen, my girl, I can hear how angry you are, but you need to help me here. What did she do? What did you do? What happened...?"

Emma took a minute to think back over her day. It hurt to

have to do it, but finally she got to the part she knew would show her mom what the "pointy lady" was all about.

"We were supposed to have gym today – it's day 3 and we always have gym on day 3 – but Donny Howard was fooling around like he always does and so she wouldn't let any of us have gym. It's not fair!" Emma spat out the final three words with a viciousness that startled Julianna. Where was the calm, happy Emma she had sent out the door this morning?

"I agree that that wasn't much fun for you, but Miss Glass must have had her reasons for doing what she did," Julianna ventured.

"But Donny always fools around. We'll never get gym again!" Emma moaned. Sulking, she concentrated for a minute on the chocolate chip cookie she was munching. Then she continued, "And you should see how much homework she gave us. Mrs. Harvey only gives us spelling, but the pointy lady gave us so much math and social studies that no one could get it done in class. I've got hours and hours of work tonight!" Emma's moaning was intensifying.

"The pointy lady?" Julianna had to hold back a smile when she heard Emma's pet name for Miss Glass.

"You should see her, Mom," Emma explained. "If you bumped into her by mistake, you'd get cut. I'm not kidding!"

"So she's – uh, pointy, she took away your gym class, and she gave you lots of work, and because of all that, you're not going back to school?"

Emma didn't know how to explain how Miss Glass made her feel inside. Sighing, she continued, "She picked on me, Mom. Not just that one time, but all day long. I thought at first that it was only me, but we were talking about it in the playground, and all the kids felt the same way. She yells at us for everything! Donny asked me if he could borrow a pencil, and she yelled at us for talking."

"She should have been ecstatic that Donny wanted to write something down, shouldn't she?" Julianna laughed.

"I told her that, Mom, but she thought I was being 'interperbent', or something like that. I don't know what it means, but it didn't sound good."

"Impertinent?"

"Yeah, I think that was it. What does it mean anyway?" Emma asked.

It was just at that moment that Peter burst through the door with his friend Bobby Pastorelli, who came to the Solomons' often after school when his mother was at work. "Hi Mom, can we have a snack?" Peter asked in his usual straight-to-the-point fashion.

"Magic word?" Julianna and Emma both said as a reflex. Peter's manners were a family project.

"Please, pretty please, please, please, please," Peter said, with an impish grin. *Why can't he just say it the first time?* his mother wondered, while his sister asked herself, *Why can't he just say it once, like a normal brother?*

"Of course," Julianna said, getting up and moving to organize their snack. "I'd like you two to take your snack into the family room today, though, please. Emma and I are talking."

"Oh yeah. What about?" Peter wanted to know.

"My new teacher," said Emma.

"Is she the one who looks like Cruella DeVil from *101 Dalmations*?" Bobby's assessment of "the pointy lady" was just what Emma needed to break her sulky mood. She burst out laughing!

"Yeah, that's the one! She acts like Cruella DeVil, too! That's what Mom and I are talking about."

"We had her for music today," Peter said. "She made us write stuff out. We never write stuff out in music. We just sing and do clapping games usually. She was no fun. Anyway, Bobby, let's go. Can we watch TV with our snack?"

"Magic word?" This time, Bobby had joined the chorus.

"PLEASE!"

"Yes, you may – but please be careful with your food. And bring your plates back when you're done."

After the boys left, Julianna looked back at her daughter. "Now, where were we? Oh, yes, you were being impertinent."

"But I wasn't, Mom. At least, I don't think I was!" Emma insisted. "I was just offering a helpful suggestion, just like you're always telling us to do!"

"Your heart was in the right place, probably, Emma, but do you think there might have been something mean about the way you said the words?"

Emma thought about that, and then shook her head. "I don't think so, Mom, but she sure got mad. And after that, nothing I did all day was good enough."

"You said you missed recess?" Julianna queried.

"Yeah, this afternoon. Some people from the choir came to get books for practicing at home, and I knew where Mrs. Harvey had put them, so I got up and got them. Miss Glass yelled at me to sit down and made me stay in at recess," Emma explained.

"I'm guessing there's more to the story than that, honey," Julianna ventured. "Did Miss Glass ask you for your help?"

"No," Emma answered, "but you're always telling us to volunteer to be of help to people. That's what I thought I was doing."

"Uh huh. How do you think Miss Glass saw it?" Julianna wondered.

"Well, the kids were pretty bad today, with Mrs. Harvey away and all," Emma explained. "I suppose she just thought I was misbehaving, getting out of my seat without asking."

"Bingo," said Julianna, who had occasionally been a parent

volunteer and had seen some badly behaved children in the school.

After hearing a whole day's worth of similar stories, Julianna was torn. She knew it was important that teachers and parents work together, and that she should support the actions of the teacher in the classroom. But this Miss Glass sounded as if she had it in for Emma – and the entire Fourth Grade class.

"Do you think I should make an appointment to see Miss Glass, Em?"

"I don't know. Well maybe... Yes... No, maybe not yet."

"Well, we'll talk about this later, Em," Julianna said. "You know I like you to work out your own solutions, but if you need me to go and talk to her, I will."

Tim and Taylor arrived just then, and the brief moment of privacy between Julianna and her younger daughter ended. Emma went off to practice her violin, and Julianna started dinner preparations.

* * *

Julianna didn't hear too much about the pointy Miss Glass for the next few days. The Solomon household was, as usual, a constant whirl of activities – music lessons, team practices, church activities – and Miss Glass didn't even get mentioned again until Friday night. And it wasn't Emma who mentioned her, but Tim.

After Emma and Peter had gone to bed, Julianna and Jake were settling down in front of a video, a Friday night tradition. Sometimes the children joined them, but tonight had been designated "adults only". Just as the two tired Solomon parents were getting comfortable on the couch in front of their movie, Tim stuck his head through the door. "Excuse me, Mom, Dad," he said, "I know this is an "adults only" night, but there's something I think I need to talk to you about. It's about Emma."

Jake reached for the controller to turn the TV off. "C'mon in, Tim," he said. "What's up?"

"Well...." It was hard for Tim to get started. "I don't like to be a tattle-tale, but I've thought and thought about this, and I think you guys would want to know." Tim paused.

"Yes? You've got our interest, son," Jake encouraged.

"Well, you know that new teacher who's taking Mrs. Harvey's place right now?"

"Ah yes," remarked Julianna, "the pointy Miss Glass." Julianna had told Jake about her conversation with Emma earlier in the week. "I haven't heard anything from Emma since that day she came home in tears. I thought things had worked themselves out."

"Not exactly, Mom," Tim replied. "The kids really hate her, and they've caused her a lot of trouble. And guess who's the ringleader?"

"Not Emma...," Julianna said hesitantly.

"Yes, Emma. That's what I hear anyway. Some of my friends have kid sisters and brothers in that class, and they say Emma and Cathy Parker have led a kind of revolt. They call it the "We're Not Doing It Club". Apparently, they're being nicey-nicey with her, but they're just saying, 'No, thanks, Miss Glass, we're not doing it' if they think there is too much work."

"I can't believe it," Julianna said, in shock. "This sounds like something Cathy Parker might think of, but Emma? It doesn't sound like our Emma, does it?"

"No, it doesn't," replied Jake. "But we hear so little from her around here, it's hard to say."

"I hope I was right to tell you," Tim said, on his way back up to his room. "I don't like to get Em in trouble, but there's something not right about what she's doing."

"You bet there is," Jake answered, Julianna nodding her agreement. "You did the right thing. Tough to be a big brother sometimes, isn't it?" The Friday night movie would have to wait, as Julianna reached for the big family Bible that sat on the coffee table in the family room.

* * *

Emma knew something was up the minute she came down to breakfast the next morning. Taylor was playing in a basketball tournament, and Tim had volunteered to be scorekeeper, so both of them were up and out of the house before Emma made her appearance. Peter was happily watching Saturday morning cartoons. The tip-off that things were not "normal", if they ever were at the Solomon house, was the stony looks on her parents' faces as they said their good mornings to her. It felt mighty frosty in the Solomon kitchen.

It's probably none of my business, Emma thought to herself, popping two slices of bread in the toaster, *so I'll just eat my breakfast fast and head back upstairs to do my homework. Oh, I forgot, I'm not doing my homework. Good! I can get my practicing out of the way instead. I wonder what's bugging Mom and Dad?*

Emma's thoughts came to an abrupt halt, when her father said her name, and not in his usual kind tone either. "Emma," Jake repeated. "Your mother and I have some concerns about school, and we were hoping you could explain some things to us."

Emma was surprised. She hadn't said a word about school to anyone in the family. She was handling it herself, just like she was supposed to do. "Sure, Dad, I guess so." Emma's toast popped, and she reached for the peanut butter and a knife.

"We were wondering how things were going with Miss Glass. You've been so quiet about her," her dad continued.

"Better." Emma busied herself spreading peanut butter on her toast. *What is this about?* She wondered.

"Better? What does that mean, exactly?" Julianna wondered.

27

"I remember you in tears telling me about how she picked on you and how much work she was giving you. You were so upset when she first arrived, and since then we've heard nothing. Does that mean you like her now?"

"Oh no," Emma said. That vicious tone that Julianna had heard when they had talked about Miss Glass before had crept into Emma's voice again. "She's awful. But we're taking care of it."

"You're taking care of it?" Jake repeated. He had taken off his glasses and was tapping them on the table, which always put Emma on edge. Emma pushed her toast away nervously.

Until now, Emma had felt proud of how she and her friends had found a way to deal with Miss Glass. She had felt grown up and responsible – and she had managed to get Cathy Parker to stop criticizing her all the time. Donny Howard seemed to think she was pretty cool, too. But now, seeing her dad's expression, she didn't feel proud or responsible anymore. Suddenly, Emma knew in her heart that she had let her parents down.

Emma sat quiet, looking down at her hands in her lap.

"Well?" This one-word question was her mother's way of insisting on an answer.

"Well, what?"

"Well, how are you taking care of it? We need to know about the "We're Not Doing It Club.""

"You wouldn't understand."

"Excuse me, young lady." Jake Solomon was shocked at his daughter's tone. "You will not speak to your mother that way. She's asking for an explanation of the Club you and Cathy Parker have organized, and we're both waiting for your answer."

There was a short silence as Emma tried to think of how she would explain the Club to her parents. She knew she could avoid it no longer. "Well," Emma began slowly, "Miss Glass was dumping so much work on us, and yelling at us so much.

So we talked about it at recess, some of the kids and I, and we thought up this idea, that if none of us would do it she couldn't really punish us all. Somehow, Cathy and I became the leaders – I don't exactly know how – but Cathy would decide what she thought was fair, and I figured out a way to spread the word to the rest of the class. It's pretty cool, really; and so far Miss Glass doesn't know what's happening, I don't think. We're all acting very polite, but we're not finishing her work. I think she just thinks we're a slow class."

"And this is making class better?" Jake asked.

"Not really. She still yells at us, and she thinks we're stupid. And if you ask me, Cathy puts the limits way too low, so it's kind of boring. But at least Miss Glass isn't pushing us around as much as she did. And we took care of it ourselves, Mom, just like you told me to."

"I told you to do this?" Julianna was very angry, but also disappointed in herself. She knew she should have found out about this much sooner. "I told you to openly disobey your teacher and lead others to do so as well?"

Emma's shoulders slumped and she sheepishly looked down at her hands again. "I didn't think of it that way, Mom."

"What were you thinking? Please explain it to us, young lady," Jake interjected.

"Well, Miss Glass is so mean, and we don't understand her when she teaches us something, and we miss Mrs. Harvey, and we had to do something. And besides, for a while Cathy Parker isn't being mean to me, and Donny Howard likes me, too. Kids usually think I'm such a loser because I never do anything wrong."

"So, let me get this straight," Julianna said. "This is about Miss Glass, Mrs. Harvey, Cathy Parker, and Donny Howard? Emma, aren't you forgetting someone? What would Jesus be saying to you if he were here with us now?"

"Wouldn't Jesus want me to get along with everyone? I don't usually get along very well with Cathy and Donny."

"Yes, of course, he wants you to get along, but not if you have to sin in order to do it. Then you must do the right thing, even if it means giving up the approval of your two new friends."

"You know, Emma, your mother and I puzzled over this last night when we heard about what was happening, and we looked in the Bible. It seems to us that this is all about what's called authority, and as a Christian it is up to us to submit to authority. That is, if someone has been put in charge of us, we are to trust that God has a reason for putting them in that position, and so we must simply obey. Miss Glass is in charge of you, and my Principal is my boss so he's in charge of me. Your mother and I are in charge of all you children, and we require obedience from you. But you know whom we work for? The Heavenly Father. We submit to him as we try to make good decisions about you. It's a lot more complicated than that, but what you need to know is that it's not your job to "take care of it:" as you said you and your friends were doing. It's your job to do as Miss Glass sets out for you, as best you can, as pleasantly as you can. That's God's way."

"You know I'm a big fan of Solomon," Julianna picked up from her husband. "So I'll share a few Proverbs that deal with what you're going through. Here's one: 'Whoever loves discipline loves knowledge, but he who hates correction is stupid.' Tough words! Do you want God to think you're stupid? I hope not! Here's another: 'When a man's ways are pleasing to the Lord, he makes even his enemies live at peace with him.' Don't you think the rest of the year will be better for you all if you make peace with your new teacher? In Leviticus, we found this: 'Rise in the presence of the aged, show respect for the elderly and revere your God'. You see, God expects us to respect people who are older than we are, so that adds to the reasons why you must learn to get along with your new teacher."

"But Mom, she's so mean. Do you really think we're just supposed to take it? Cathy says it's not fair and we have rights and we don't have to put up with it."

"We looked and we looked for permission to do what you have done," Julianna explained.

"Daniel disobeyed his king, but only because he was being asked to worship in a way he knew was against God's law. Apart from a situation like that, though, nowhere are we given permission for disrespect or defiance of our leaders. Here's what we found: "The eyes of the Lord are everywhere, keeping watch on the wicked and the good." Don't you think God loves Miss Glass too? Don't you think he knows what's going on in your classroom? Don't you think he can make good things happen?"

"Here's something else we noticed last night that we hadn't seen before in all the times we have read about David. Do you remember about Saul and how he felt about David after David became a popular leader of Israel?"

"He was jealous of him, wasn't he?"

"Yes, he was. And much worse. On several occasions, Saul threw his spear at David in an attempt to kill him. And do you know how David treated Saul after that? Did he try to kill Saul to defend himself? No. David's attitude did not change. Saul was his King, anointed by God, and David knew he was to serve him. Later, when David and Saul were at war, David had several chances to kill Saul, but David always chose to spare him. So, I think if David can spare a man who tried to kill him several times, then you can spare Miss Glass."

Emma nodded in agreement, but she remained silent.

"What are you thinking, Em?" her dad asked.

"I'm thinking about how ungrateful Saul was. David killed

Goliath for him, didn't he? And David could still be nice to him. That's cool. But..."

"But what?" Julianna asked.

"What do I do about the 'We're Not Doing It Club'?"

"Hand in your resignation?" Jake suggested.

* * *

All day Monday, Julianna had a very hard time concentrating on the drawings she was supposed to be doing for the Parkesville Little Theater. Her mind kept going back to the drama that must be playing itself out in Miss Glass' classroom. She wondered how the leading lady, her Emma, was surviving the challenge of removing herself from the 'We're Not Doing It Club'. Emma was surrounded by children who didn't know that such defiance was wrong; children who had their own ways of getting even when they felt betrayed. Emma was faced with a teacher who was, so far, hard to respect. Tough things for a fourth grader. Julianna talked to God about it several times that day.

The Emma who came through the door that afternoon was the Emma Julianna remembered from before the Miss Glass incident. She was smiling and cheerful, though not too talkative. She brought Angela Pastorelli home with her after school. (Angela was Bobby's big sister, and Emma's best friend.)

"So, Emma, how was your day?" Julianna asked as the two girls bustled through the door.

"Good." Things were back to normal; Julianna had to pry information from her younger daughter.

"C'mon, Em, you know what I mean," her mother persisted. "What happened with you and the 'We're Not Doing It Club'?"

"Oh that," Emma said vaguely. "Well, I just stopped sending the signals Cathy wanted me to send. At morning recess, she cornered me in the yard, but I just said I wasn't playing along anymore. I told her I was giving Miss Glass a chance. She was pretty mad at me, so she said some bad stuff and went off in search of a new partner. So I'm in her bad books again, but you know – I don't care. I know I feel better about me now. And what do I care what she thinks about me? I've got Ange."

Julianna looked toward Angela, who was just watching and smiling. "Speaking for Angela and myself," Julianna put in happily, "we're glad to have the real Emma back. That other one was pretty scary." She hugged her daughter. "So how was Miss Glass today?"

"I don't know, Mom. She seemed different. Not so mean. She was actually wearing red today instead of black, but she almost seemed nice. And I got all my work done. I even caught her smiling once. Amazing, eh?"

"Amazing. That's God's way, Emma!"

And Julianna and her two young friends celebrated with milk and fresh-baked cookies the wisdom of a young Solomon, who had learned the value of submission and respect for God's leaders.

ADVISORS
(Proverbs 15:22 / 16:3)

Taylor Solomon was so excited that she jumped over the tulips that were just beginning to bloom along the Solomons' front walk. Then she rushed into the house, disentangling her long blond hair from her baseball cap as she ran. She was just coming home on a Saturday afternoon after her Crusaders meeting, and she was bursting to tell her mom about the carnival she had volunteered to organize.

Taylor wanted to get started right away, and she always ran new ideas past her mother. Julianna Solomon was always full of suggestions for her children's projects. But where was she? Taylor called out to her, and looked for her in all her usual places, but no luck.

Then Taylor remembered: her mom had been asked to present a proposal for a mural to decorate the new French restaurant that was soon opening in downtown Parkesville. That meant that she was probably up in the third floor studio where she always went to work on her contracts as an artist. When Mom was working, there was a strict rule that the children should not interrupt unless there was blood spurting somewhere. This was especially true for Taylor and her twin brother Tim, who, at twelve, were the oldest of the Solomon children and, therefore, expected to be examples for their younger siblings, nine-year-old Emma and seven-year-old Peter. But Taylor was so excited about her news that she just knew her mom would understand.

Her mom did *not* understand. When Taylor knocked on the studio door and let herself in, she was met by an expression she seldom witnessed on her mother's face: anger mixed with

35

frustration. If Julianna Solomon were a cartoon character, there would be storm clouds circling around her head. Taylor immediately regretted having set foot in the studio, but now that she was there she thought she should explain her mission. "Mom, I'm sorry to bother you, but..."

Taylor's mother looked out at her over the top of her glasses, and her eyes seemed to say, "This had better be good."

Taylor forged ahead. "...we're having a carnival at the church to raise money for the Smythes–you know, the missionaries we sponsor over in South Africa. Well, you know how I've always wanted to be a missionary and I thought this would be a good way for me to learn about it, and so I volunteered to run the committee. Now that I have the job, I was hoping I could talk to you about it." After blurting out her news as quickly as she could, Taylor paused to take a breath.

"Taylor, I'm proud of you, really I am," her mom replied, "but right now I have challenges of my own. I have to have a proposal ready for the mural at the Vive la France Restaurant by tomorrow, and I just can't find an idea that works."

"When I think of a French restaurant," Taylor suggested meekly, "I always think of the Eiffel Tower."

"Yes, yes, but I need something a little more original than that, I think," her mom said coldly. "Now please, Taylor, leave me alone. We'll have to talk later. And shut the door behind you on your way out."

Taylor slunk from the room and quietly closed the door. Then leaning her back against the door, she let out a sigh, shook her head, and said to herself, "Phew! I was lucky to get out of there alive." Taylor wasn't used to being treated so rudely by her mother, and it took away some of her enthusiasm about the carnival.

"Chocolate," she said aloud suddenly, "that's what I need to get my creative juices flowing."

Taylor made her way to the kitchen in search of the chocolate cookies she remembered seeing on the counter. Down in the kitchen, she found her father, Jake Solomon, and her twin brother, Tim. They had just come in from a baseball practice, starving as usual. Taylor pounced on the chocolate cookies before Tim and her dad could polish them all off.

Tim was pouring large glasses of cold milk. "Hey, Taylor, you want some?" he asked, always the perfect gentleman.

"Sure, thanks." Taylor smiled, reaching for one of the glasses. "How was practice?"

"It was good," her dad answered. "Your brother here was batting really well today. In fact, Tim, I wish you had saved that home run for Saturday's game."

Tim laughed. "Yeah, that would have been good. My mitt had a big hole in it, though. The less said about my catching the better. So, what happened at Crusaders today, Taylor? I hate it when they schedule Crusaders and baseball at the same time. I don't like missing either of them."

"And I know why," his sister joked. "Because we always give you the juiciest jobs when you're not there to defend yourself! Wanna know what you got 'volunteered' for this time?"

"I'm not sure. Do I?"

"You'd better sit down for this one, bro'. Guess what you get to do? You get to work for me! I love it!! For once, I get to tell you what to do, and you can't say, 'but I'm older than you' to get out of it! Ha! My chance to get even." Tim was the older of the twins, and reminding Taylor of his rank as "senior sibling" was one of his favorite ways to tease his sister. Taylor was happy to be able to put her brother in his place for once. She was prancing victoriously out of the kitchen, milk and cookies in hand.

"Now wait a minute, Tay," Tim called after her, using the

nickname he had used since early childhood. "You haven't told me what I'm doing. What's the project?"

"Oh, did I neglect that little bit of information? Sorry, Tim Tim," Taylor smirked, using her pet name for her brother. "We're having a carnival to raise money to send to the Smythes in South Africa. Isn't that exciting?!"

"That is pretty cool," Tim agreed, "but what exactly are we doing at this carnival?"

"That's what I don't know yet, and what you're going to help me to figure out."

As they were talking, Jake Solomon had left the kitchen, returning shortly with a Bible in his hand. "May I interrupt this high level planning session?" he interjected when he found what he had been looking for. "I ran across some ideas in Proverbs just this morning. I've just found the passage again. I think you'll appreciate it. 'Commit to the Lord whatever you do, and your plans will succeed.' Also, 'Plans fail for lack of counsel, but with many advisors they succeed.' Pretty good advice for carnival planning, I'd say."

"Wow!" Taylor said. "I didn't know God was interested in carnival committees! Isn't it cool how he's got something to say about everything!"

"It sure is," her dad answered, laughing.

"Well, Dad, we've already taken care of the first one. We prayed about it at Crusaders just before we came home, and I know I need to keep praying as we get organized."

"That second proverb tells you not to do it all yourself, Taylor. By choosing your 'advisors' wisely, you should get lots of ideas and lots of helpers."

"I'd like to volunteer right now for the job of 'advisor'," said Tim, chuckling. "Then I can send you a big bill at the end of it all. Right?"

"Yeah, right." Sighing deeply, Taylor wondered if she was going to survive working on a committee with her twin.

Patience, patience, she said to herself, as she headed toward the phone to get started.

"Any idea where Emma and Peter are?" Jake asked Taylor. "I think we three are on dinner duty, with your mom hiding up in her studio." Emma Solomon enjoyed helping out in the kitchen, and Peter loved stirring things–sometimes all over the counter and floor!

"How does Papa Jake's Famous Macaroni Dinner sound to you?"

"Yum!" came a chorus from both the twins. "Papa Jake" made truly excellent macaroni!

* * *

Taylor was on the upstairs hall phone when she saw her dad go up to the studio with a cup of tea for her mom.

"How's it coming, honey?" Taylor heard her dad's quiet inquiry. Taylor couldn't understand her mom's reply, but she could tell from the tone that things were still not going well with the mural. She was relieved to hear her parents share a short laugh about something, but then she could see that her dad was leaving the room.

Jake paused in the doorway of the studio to speak to his wife. "Remember that holiday we took when we were first married, to the south of France," Taylor heard him say. "That's what I always think of when I think of anything French. You know, the cafes and the beaches and all those expensive villas and yachts."

Taylor heard her mom murmur a reply, then her dad was on his way down the stairs. When he saw Taylor, he said, "Your mom is in a flap up there, eh? By the way, she's sorry about how she acted with you earlier."

"No problem. It was my fault. I forgot the Blood Spurting Rule!"

Jake Solomon was grinning as he headed back to the kitchen.

* * *

Taylor slammed down the phone. "Ooo– she can be so stubborn!" she said to no one in particular.

"Hey Taylor!" Jake Solomon called up from the kitchen. "What's happening up there?"

Taylor made her way down to the kitchen and sat at the breakfast bar. From there she could watch Peter stirring something white and gooey in the big pot on the stove. (Taylor was hopeful that Peter would keep his mind on the job for once, or she knew who would be on the cleanup crew!) Emma was pulling vegetables out of the fridge, and her dad was up to his elbows in grated cheese and the other secret ingredients in Papa Jake's Macaroni. He waved a huge knife menacingly in Taylor's direction when she helped herself to a chunk of cheese.

"So, what's up?" asked the chef, going back to his chopping.

"I've just been talking to Frannie about the carnival." Frances O'Brien was a neighbor and a friend of the Solomon children. "I called her to see if she wanted to be on the committee, but she wants everything her own way! I thought I was supposed to be in charge!"

"Who else have you talked to?" her dad asked.

"Sara Spencer. She's new in town, and I thought it would be a good way to get to know her. Then Tim suggested that I ask Ryan Barnicke to work with us too. Everyone says they'll help, but yikes! They all have different ideas about what we should do. You told me I needed advisors, but I sure don't see how it's going to work!"

"When's your first meeting going to be?" her dad asked, smiling.

"Tomorrow, after church, if that's okay with you and mom," Taylor said. "I thought we could have a picnic lunch in the backyard, and have the meeting afterward."

"You and Tim will have to take charge of the lunch arrangements yourselves. Do you think you can handle it?"

"Sure, Dad! I'll check right now for supplies."

Taylor was already rushing toward the fridge, when her dad said, "Slow down, Taylor! One more question: Will Pastor Mike be coming over too?" Pastor Mike was the youth pastor at their church.

"Oh boy, how could I forget about him?" Taylor exclaimed. "I'll call him right away, then I'll check on lunch supplies, then I'll jot down some ideas for the carnival. This is exciting! As long as my friends and my brother don't drive me crazy!" Taylor was already reaching for the church directory to look up Pastor Mike's phone number.

* * *

Later that day, the Solomon family was enjoying their delicious meal courtesy of "Papa Jake" and his two assistants. Everyone was digging in, with the exception of Julianna, who was just moving hers around on her plate with her fork.

"Ah, Mom," Peter whined, "We put the tomatoes in just for you. Don't you like it? It's good for us this way, right?"

Julianna smiled at her youngest child and was warmed by his enthusiasm. "It's yummy, Pete. You three have done a great job. I just can't get my mind off my work, I'm afraid. I've got major artist's block!"

"You want my two cents worth, Mom?" Tim asked. His mom just shrugged, so Tim pressed on. "I really like that bicycle race they have every year in France. It's exciting, and people compete from all over the world."

"The Tour de France," Jake said. "Good idea, Tim. That would appeal to the athletes who might eat in the restaurant."

Emma, the shyest of the Solomon children, spoke hesitantly. "We learned how to say 'Enjoy your food' in French at school last week. 'Bon appetit'. I think that sounds cool."

Then Peter, not to be left out, suggested, "I know, I know. What about French fries?"

They all laughed, and then went back to their food. Julianna was deep in thought. Then suddenly, she rose from the table, saying, "Sorry, guys. This is a great meal, but I'm finally getting an idea, and I'm afraid if I don't get to the drawing board right now I may lose it. Please forgive me." And she rushed out of the room.

Her family watched her leave. Then "Papa Jake" said, "Anyone for dessert? I feel like an ice cream sundae!"

The cheers from the children could be heard down the block.

* * *

Sitting down together for a big Sunday morning breakfast was a Solomon tradition. This Sunday, Tim made scrambled eggs for everyone while Taylor cooked bacon in the microwave, Emma squeezed oranges for juice, and Peter set the table. The children were thinking that perhaps this once their mom wouldn't make Sunday breakfast. She hadn't been spotted since she had so mysteriously left the table the night before.

As Jake and the kids were settling down at the breakfast bar for their bacon and eggs, though, Julianna came into the kitchen. "Good morning, everyone!" she said cheerfully. They could see that the sweet-tempered Mom they were used to had returned, and they shared a sigh of relief.

"Hey, who's this?" Jake Solomon teased his wife. "It looks like that grumpy, rude woman who rejected our dinner last night, but it can't be. This woman smiles!"

"Sorry about that. But listen. I have to thank you guys. You gave me the idea I needed."

Julianna was beaming. "I got to thinking about all the suggestions you gave me, and I came up with a collage. I figured out a way to use all of your ideas plus a few of my own to appeal to everyone's different impressions of France. Hopefully, that will make everyone feel at home at the restaurant. I'll take you all up to the studio after breakfast. But right now, I'm starving! Please pass the eggs."

Jake winked at Taylor. "See what I mean about using 'many advisors'? Maybe you can learn from your mom's experience. Open your mind at your meeting, and I'll bet good things will happen. If you trust your plans to the Lord."

"Now, what's all this?" asked Julianna between bites. "I'm obviously behind on some family business." Taylor was happy to share all the details of the carnival planning, in preparation for the meeting that afternoon after church.

* * *

Taylor and her friends were sitting around the picnic table in the shade of the Solomons' spacious back yard. Taylor was sitting between Frannie and Ryan, and opposite them were Pastor Mike, Sara, and Tim. What was left of their lunches was still on the table: some sandwiches, a plate of cookies, and some juice boxes.

Ryan was wearing brand new runners which he was using to kick Tim under the table at every opportunity. Tim was stealing and eating Ryan's food. A normal day for those two!

There had been lots of good-humored discussion over lunch about all kinds of things: their upcoming junior youth retreat, school projects, a band Tim wanted to see in concert and, of course, the carnival. Frannie had talked and talked about the carnival, and the other kids had had trouble getting a word in edgewise. Sara, as the "new kid on the block", had stayed pretty quiet.

Taylor had also been quiet–especially for her!–as she listened to the chatter and the laughter. She was wondering how to make the best of the 'advisors' God had given her. She was a bit nervous, but she knew Pastor Mike would help her out. And she had remembered to pray about the meeting. In fact, she had prayed about it almost non-stop since volunteering for the job.

Sometimes Taylor wondered why she had been so quick to open her big mouth! She loved the Smythes, and she knew some other kids would be raising money for *her* missionary work some day. But still... This was a big responsibility.

Well, no time like the present, Taylor said to herself. She took a deep breath, and said, loudly enough to be heard over the other conversations, "What do you say we start the meeting now, guys? Anybody need more juice or a cookie before we start?"

"Sure, boss," Tim piped up, as both he and Ryan helped themselves to more cookies. Taylor shot him a murderous glance. He'd really been overdoing the "boss" routine; then again, what did she expect? She had started it.

Everyone shifted a bit in their seats and waited quietly for Taylor to continue. Taylor had never seen this group so quiet and their attention rattled her. Another deep breath. "Pastor Mike, do you think we should pray?"

"You bet," replied the youth pastor through his thick brown walrus moustache. That moustache was his pride and joy, and the kids were always teasing him about it, as did his wife, Kim. "Do you want me to do it?" Taylor saw him wink, and knew he was trying to take the pressure off her a bit. Pastor Mike was totally cool, and seemed to be able to tune in to the kids better than most adults.

"Thanks, Pastor Mike, that'd be great." Taylor smiled.

"Heavenly Father, thank you for these young people who have risen to the challenge of helping the Smythes to serve you in South Africa. Please bless and guide their efforts, and help them to bring glory to your name. Help them to work together, to listen to each other, to share and to build on each other's ideas, and to have fun. In Jesus' name. Amen." Pastor Mike paused, then he looked at Taylor and said, "Over to you, boss."

"Okay, guys," Taylor began. "We're here to come up with good plans to make some money for the Smythes. I know we all have different ideas about what we'd like to have at the carnival, and I don't see why we can't do it all. What I thought was that we should just go around the table and tell the group the one activity you think the carnival has to have. I'll write down your suggestions, and we'll decide as a group which ones to do." She looked to her left. "Why don't you start, Frannie?"

"Well, as I've already said, I think we should have a DJ, a raffle, one of those bouncing castles for the little kids, lots of food, and a dart game where you can win prizes. I also think..."

"Slow down there, kiddo," Taylor said quickly when Frannie paused to take a breath. "You only get one suggestion on the first round. So what would be the ONE suggestion you think is really the best?"

Frannie thought for a moment. "Just one? That's hard. Okay. I remember going to a carnival like this when I was a kid, and my absolute favorite thing was the bouncing castle. I know my little brother would love it, and probably Peter and his friends too. And if the kids want to come, then their parents have to come too, so we get lots of people. Yup, that's my best suggestion."

"Great," said Taylor as she wrote Bouncing Castle on her list. "But how do we get one of those?"

"That's where I come in," Pastor Mike piped up. "I get on the phone with my mellowest tones, and I talk someone into a deal we can afford. I'll try anyway. Leave that with me."

Sara was next to make her suggestion. "We had a carnival at my church in Whitby, and do you know what made the most money for us? Cotton candy! My mom can probably tell us where to get the equipment."

"Do you think they'd deliver all the way to little old Parkesville, Sara?" Pastor Mike asked.

"I don't know, but my mom would be glad to find out."

"Another great idea for our list," Taylor said, writing.

"May I make a suggestion, Taylor?" Pastor Mike offered. "Don't forget to record who has agreed to find out what information, so you can nag us about it later. I'll do my best, but I do need lots of nagging. Just ask Pastor Ron. And my wife, for that matter."

The kids laughed. Then Tim piped up. "I think we should organize a baseball tournament – maybe kids versus their parents, or families versus families. Do you think we could do that, Pastor Mike?"

"Oh no, another job! I'll contact the school beside the church and see if we can use their field the day of the carnival. A tournament will take lots of organization, you know, but what a way to get all the members of the church involved! I guess I'd better start warming up my pitching arm..."

"You'll never get it past Tim and me, though," bragged Ryan. "We're hot this year!"

"Yeah, right," all the girls said in unison, rolling their eyes and laughing.

"My turn," Ryan went on. "You guys have missed the absolute best, most stupendous, totally amazing idea! We've just got to have a dunk tank. You know, where people sit on a seat above a tank of water and other people throw a ball to try to make them fall into the water. It's so funny! I can just see your dad up there, Tim. Or Ms. Shaw." Ms. Shaw was the principal of their school and a member of their church. "And then again, there's everybody's favorite – Pastor Mike." All the kids looked at Pastor Mike, who was rolling his eyes skyward and whistling tunelessly, hoping not to be noticed.

"No way," he protested. "You don't want to see me in my swim trunks. Really, you don't. Not safe for women and children. Or you guys either!"

Everyone laughed. "We'll risk it!" Taylor said, as she added the dunk tank to her list. "What a great start! Now who's got another suggestion? Why don't we go around the table the other way this time? Ryan, your turn again."

After they had each had two more turns, they had a very impressive list of activities. They had to veto Ryan's suggestion of mud wrestling. They also thought that Frannie's suggestion about a hot air balloon might be a bit too expensive. In addition to their first round suggestions, though, they had lots of ideas they could work with: a fish pond, a dart game, apple bobbing, decorate-your-own cupcakes, a Christian DJ, a hot dog and hamburger barbeque, arts and crafts for the kids, and a few others. It was going to be great!

Through the discussion, each of the committee members became responsible for some follow-up activities, and everyone was to report to Taylor when they made progress. The kids knew they had taken on a huge project, and they only had a month before the carnival was scheduled; but now they knew that with good planning, cooperation, and support from lots of volunteers at the church, they could pull it off!

* * *

The day of the carnival dawned bright and sunny. Taylor and Tim knew that because they were up at 5 a.m. putting finishing touches on their preparations for the big day. They were meeting the other members of the committee at the church at 7 to start putting up the booths.

All of their hard work paid off! The carnival was a smashing success. Taylor tried to be everywhere at once, making sure everyone had a good time. They did!

Jake had been convinced to be DJ for the day, and shocked some of his students from the high school with the wild and crazy side of his personality. The bouncing castle was busy all morning with happy youngsters safely bumping into each other to their hearts' content. People enjoyed a wonderful barbeque prepared by the men and women of the church. Pastor Mike was a sensation in the dunk tank, praising the Lord and practically emptying the tank each time someone hit the target. Tim and Ryan were on the winning team in the softball tournament.

Taylor and her committee members went home sunburnt and exhausted but pleased with themselves, and they had made over $500 for the Smythes' mission.

That night at the Solomon home, the family ordered a celebration dinner from Taylor's favorite Chinese take-out, Woo's. Taylor's fortune cookie read, "All your plans shall prosper." Who could disagree with that? The Solomons were happy to celebrate the wisdom of a young Solomon, who had learned to entrust her plans to the Lord and to use the advice of others instead of carrying the whole burden herself.

TWICE THE VICTORY
(Proverbs 29: 11)

Tim Solomon chomped down on a huge spoonful of sweet cereal as his twelve-year-old twin sister shook the empty cereal box.

"Mom," Taylor Solomon whined, "Tim's taken the last of the Cinnamon Crunchies again!"

"Well, I deserve them more than you do. I am older than you, after all, and I have to play in a big game today," answered Tim in between bites.

"Older than me? Five minutes older, you mean. I don't think that counts." The Solomon twins often had this argument. Tim had been born before his sister, and he loved to rub it in every chance he got.

"Being the older twin should have earned Esau the birthright, and what's good enough for the Bible is good enough for me," Tim insisted annoyingly. He grinned at his sister as he poured more milk on the treasured cereal and then dug his spoon once more into the huge pile of crispy squares in his bowl.

"Yeah, but we both know how that story worked out: Jacob got the birthright and became the father of the Israelite nation. So there, big brother!" Taylor shot back. Then she turned back to her mother. "Look how much he took, Mom. There's enough there to feed half of the starving children in the world, let alone his two hungry siblings here in Parkesville. Poor Emma is sitting here starving too, and he's just helped himself to the whole box."

Julianna Solomon was leaning against the counter opposite the breakfast bar in their sunny kitchen, where three of her four

49

little "angels" sat having breakfast – or at least arguing about having breakfast. Emma was sleepily wiping her eyes, content for the moment to let Taylor fight her battle for her. Peter was miraculously still in bed, it seemed. Usually on Saturday mornings, he bounded out of bed at 6 to watch TV uninterrupted, but not today. Jake Solomon was already in his study marking yet another set of high school writing assignments.

"Slow down, you two," Julianna laughed. "If you'd stop bickering for just one minute, you'd figure out that I always keep an extra box of that precious stuff down in the storage cupboard . Tim, please run down to get it. Your cereal may be a little soggy when you get back, but perhaps that will remind you that you should share with your sisters."

"Sorry, Mom," Tim said, as he left the table, "but I keep thinking about the game today. We're playing the Whitby Whirlwinds. Remember the last time we played them?"

As Tim went down to the basement on his errand, he couldn't help replaying that terrible game in his mind.

* * *

It had been a sweltering July day, at the beginning of summer holidays. Baseball season had started in early May, and Tim's team, the Parkesville Panthers, had an excellent record. In fact, they hadn't lost a single league game. The boys were confident of yet another success, since they had been playing well all season. Coach Blackwood proudly called them his "well-oiled machine".

Their confidence began to fade when the Whitby pitcher, Toby Wilde, approached the mound. He was at least a head taller than everyone on the Parkesville team. Rumor had it that he had had to get his uniform specially made to fit his muscles and all the peculiar moves he used when he pitched. No wonder the other Parkesville team, the Prowlers, had nicknamed him "Wild Toby". As Tim watched Toby approach the pitcher's mound, he couldn't help feeling a bit like David about to face Goliath.

The Panthers knew they were in trouble from the first pitch. Tim's good friend, Ryan Barnicke, their lead-off batter, was usually to be counted on for at least a single, but that day he couldn't even see the ball! There were three strikes on him before he knew what was happening. As he walked back to the bench uncertainly, he was shaking his head and muttering to himself.

One by one, Tim's teammates experienced a similar fate. Even Buzz Baxter with his .495 batting average had no success that day. They just couldn't hit any of Toby's impressive variety of pitches. And the constant murmurings from catcher Alec Routledge didn't help.

After five innings of a six-inning game, the Panthers were behind by four runs. The score was an embarrassing 4 to 0. No doubt about it: their poor batting record was making them all lose confidence. Worse than that, all the players were becoming more and more frustrated and angry with themselves.

Coach Blackwood relied on Tim, who was team captain, to encourage his teammates. Tim was usually calm and collected and could be counted on to play his best, urging the others to work hard as well. But that day was not Tim's best day, by a long shot.

What Coach didn't know, and what the boys didn't want to tell him, was that although "Wild Toby"and the other players on the Whitby team were nice guys and good sports, the catcher for the Whirlwind, Alec Routledge, made a habit of saying rude things under his breath just as the ball was crossing the plate. Now, sometimes a bit of good natured teasing goes on between opposing teams, but this Alec guy went way too far, over and over!

It was Tim's turn at bat. He'd been to the plate twice before without getting a hit. His first turn had been a disaster: three quick strikes, and he was out. The second time he had actually got a piece of the ball twice, but both times the ball had gone foul. Then Toby had pitched a fast ball strike, and he was out again. This would probably be his last chance, and as captain he really felt the responsibility to do well.

Tim walked slowly to the plate, determined to hit the ball no matter what that turkey behind the plate said under his breath. But Tim had to admit to himself that he was rattled by the pressure and by the catcher's annoying comments. *Oh well,* he thought, *I can do it. I just have to stay calm. But man, he's really getting to me!*

Tim could see his mom in the stands. She never missed a game. Taylor, Emma, and Peter were there too, and he could hear Taylor yelling encouragements over the noise of the rest of the crowd. She might be annoying at home sometimes, but he had to admit that she was his number one fan at sporting events–when they weren't competing against each other, that is. Emma and Pete looked pretty hopeful too, and Tim didn't want to disappoint them. Tim's dad was unfortunately at home marking papers; but Tim knew that his dad would want to hear all about the game as soon as they got home.

All of this was swirling around in Tim's head as he walked to the plate in his most confident-looking swagger. This was it: his chance to be a hero, as his Grandpa McNab always said.

Tim calmly forced himself to look Toby straight in the eye and then he concentrated on the ball. As Toby wound up for the pitch, though, Tim heard Alec muttering behind him. "Loser, loser, loser," Alec purred. His voice was just loud enough for Tim but not the umpire to hear him. The ball went flying past Tim and into Alec's glove. Strike one.

Okay, okay, Tim said to himself, stay calm. Don't let that little weasel Routledge throw you. He tried to shake the tension out of his shoulders and set himself up for the next pitch. He would be so proud to whack one of those pitches out of the park! He was ready and waiting.

Toby let the pitch go. It was coming in fast, and it was high and outside, just where Tim liked them. But just as Tim began his swing, he heard Alec whisper hoarsely, "Wimp. Useless bunch of wimps." Tim hit the ball, but he fouled it out past the first baseman. Again, only Tim could hear Alec's insults, although Tim's buddies on the bench knew what was going on. Tim couldn't resist turning around to stare hotly at the catcher. Alec's red hair was jutting outside the catcher's mask and his eyes were bright and fiery, but otherwise he looked a picture of innocence to all the adults around. How did he manage it? Tim wondered.

It was much harder this time for Tim to collect himself. He could feel his temper building up inside him. He felt so trapped. He knew that what Alec was doing was totally against the rules; but he also knew that his teammates had a code of dealing with their own problems, rather than running to their parents and Coach for help all the time. So Tim just had to settle himself down and get on with the next pitch. He grit his teeth and tried to concentrate on the ball and the home run he was going to get.

This time Toby sent one of his famous fast balls, the kind that were so fast you couldn't see them. Alec had been stared into silence, but that didn't prevent Tim from getting his third strike. He took a deep breath to control his disappointment and his temper, but he made the mistake of looking back at Alec. Alec had stood up and removed his catcher's mask and was smirking in Tim's direction. That did it. Tim just lost it! He grabbed Alec by the shoulders, and shook him, saying, "That was all your fault, Routledge! You're ruining this whole game!" Then Tim pushed Alec so hard that Alec lost his balance and fell backwards, narrowly missing the backstop with his head. The crowd gasped when they heard the sound of Alec's head hitting the ground. Alec lay there, absolutely still.

Tim, seeing what he had done, dropped immediately to his knees beside Alec to see how he was. The two coaches rushed over as well, and pushed Tim aside to take a look. Alec's parents hurried down from their places in the stands, and there was a flurry of activity as Alec's coach checked Alec's vital signs. "He's breathing," he yelled, "but we'd better get him to hospital. Does anyone have a cell phone to call an ambulance?"

One of the parents made the call, and it wasn't too long before the paramedics arrived to take charge.

Tim was in a daze, and went straight to his room when they got back from the game. From his room he heard the muffled voices of his mom and his sisters as they soberly told the story to Tim's dad. Tim knew that his dad was shocked and disappointed by the news. Good, thought Tim, now he'll come upstairs and yell at me. Maybe then I'll feel better.

But neither of his parents came upstairs to punish Tim. Instead he heard his dad leading his family in prayer, and Tim knew he would be praying for Alec, for Alec's family, and for his doctors.

Then the house became quieter than it had ever been, as they all waited for news about the accident. Tim was left alone with his own thoughts and with his guilt.

Tim heard the phone ring at about 8 o'clock that night. He heard his mom pick up the phone, but he couldn't hear what was being said. He got up off his bed and walked anxiously to the window, afraid of the news he might receive.

Julianna found Tim staring out his bedroom window. "That was Coach Blackwood, Tim," she said. "Alec is okay."

Tim let out a sigh as he slumped down onto his bed and rested his head in his hands.

"They sent him home from hospital with a headache and a goose egg on the back of his head, but otherwise there was no damage," his mother continued. "And what's this about Alec bugging you from behind the plate?"

It was a few minutes before he could speak. "I could have really hurt him, Mom. I keep going over it and over it in my mind. I wanted so much to get a hit, and he was saying all those mean things. Then I got so mad, I couldn't even think. I just went after him. I couldn't control myself. I feel so bad, Mom. I've decided to quit baseball. I can't play if I'm going to hurt people all the time."

"Whoa, whoa there, bud," his mom said kindly. "I think you're being a little hard on yourself. Has this ever happened before?"

"Well, not exactly. I do get mad a lot, but not usually like today."

"Are you sorry about what happened?"

"Of course! What I did was awful!"

"Well then, it's obvious to me that your heart is in the right place, and that next time you will handle things differently. You've made a mistake, but you've learned from it. And God has already forgiven you, so I think you should forgive yourself." She paused to let him think about that. Then she asked, "So, what are you going to do?"

"I dunno," answered Tim. "I guess I'll start by calling Alec to apologize. Should I do that right now, do you think?"

"I think tomorrow will be soon enough for that, son," said Jake, who had just come into Tim's room to see how he was doing.

"That's a good start, honey," said Julianna, smiling at her son. "What else do you think you could do, if you ever feel yourself losing your temper like that again?"

"I guess maybe I should have talked to Coach Blackwood about Alec, instead of keeping it to myself."

"Good idea," said Tim's dad. "There are times when you need to realize that you can't handle everything on your own.

Your mom and I have to get help from other people sometimes too. And from God. Do you know what God has to say about anger, Tim? Among other things, He says, 'A fool gives full vent to his anger but a wise man keeps himself under control.' That's in Proverbs. In my work at school, I have to remind myself about this verse a lot some days, when the kids are driving me crazy. I know that if I lose my temper, I'll only make things worse. And that's what happened to you today, isn't it?"

Tim nodded.

"It's okay to be angry sometimes, Tim," his mom continued. "God knows that anger is part of being human. But the apostle Paul tells us in Ephesians, 'In your anger do not sin'. God expects us to control ourselves when those feelings start to control us. It's tough, but do you think you can try?"

Tim nodded again. "Okay," he said, as his parents came close to give him a hug.

* * *

When Tim came back to the kitchen with the Cinnamon Crunchies, he was deep in thought, and they could guess that he wasn't thinking about breakfast cereal!

"I've been thinking, Mom. About what you and Dad said to me after that last game and that big mess I made of things. I'm going to remember what God says about anger, and try to keep myself under control. Do you think I can manage it, if Alec is back to his old tricks?"

"I'm sure you can, with God's help," his mom smiled.

Just then, they heard the voices of Jake and Peter just outside the kitchen. "Now, Dad?" whispered Peter, giggling. "Now!" Jake replied.

"Ta daa!" they both chimed in as they bolted into the kitchen. They were wearing bright green T-shirts. Printed on the front of the shirts was "Tim Solomon Fan Club". Jake had shirts for Julianna and the girls as well. "That's the worst color I've ever seen," laughed Tim's mom, "but I'll be proud to wear it!"

Tim punched his dad and his little brother playfully, and grinned from ear to ear.

* * *

When Tim and his family arrived at the ball diamond, they found out that there had been some changes to the Whitby team. A new player named Gerry Latimer was replacing Alec Routledge as catcher, and Alec was playing out in right field. Alec's coach had decided to make the change. Alec had been warned about his behavior, but his coach couldn't trust him to cooperate, so he had moved him to the outfield. Everyone could see that Alec wasn't pleased about it, but what could he do?

Tim and the Panthers were really up for this game! In the three weeks since their last game against the Whitby team, Coach Blackwood had been working hard with them on hitting fast balls like the one Toby Wilde could throw, and they felt that without Alec there ruining their concentration they would have a really good shot at winning this game.

At first, everything went well. Ryan Barnicke's first at-bat got him a double, and later in the inning Buzz Baxter's single had been enough for Ryan to score the first run. And that was just the beginning!

By the sixth inning, the score was Parkesville 6, Whitby 2. The Panthers thought they had the game in the bag. Whitby was at bat, and the bases were loaded, but Tim and his teammates weren't too worried because there were already two outs. Just one more out and the game was theirs. The Whirlwinds' only possibility was a grand slam home run, and what chance was there of that?!

Gerry Latimer came up to the plate. He had turned out to be a pretty good catcher, but his batting hadn't been too impressive up to now, so Tim was pretty confident that they could handle whatever hits he could make. Their pitcher, Jimmy "Ace" Williams, threw out his first pitch. Gerry let it go by him for his first strike. The second pitch was outside for ball one. By this time there was a lot of shouting from the stands: the Whitby parents were cheering Gerry on while the Parkesville fans shouted encouragements to Ace.

Poor Gerry; everyone could see that the pressure was getting to him. Sweat dripped down his forehead through his brown bangs, and he had to brush both sweat and hair out of his eyes several times.

Then came the next pitch. Something strange came over Gerry as he watched it coming. He straightened up a bit, relaxed, and swung. The crack of the bat as it connected with the ball could be heard all the way to Whitby, 10 miles down the road! The ball sailed up over the trees and out of the park. The Whitby fans were on their feet cheering the runners. It was a grand slam homer at just the right time!

As Gerry jogged away from the plate, his ear-to-ear grin showed how proud he was. He couldn't resist making good-natured comments to the Parkesville players as he ran past them around the bases. Then he turned his head to wave to his parents in the stands, and somehow twisted his ankle. He lurched forward and just barely stayed on his feet. His grin turned to a grimace of pain, and his jog to a hobble. It was clear to all who saw him that the hero of the day was out of the game for a while.

The Whitby team's third out came shortly after Gerry had been helped off the field and given first aid. The score was now 6 to 6, and the pressure was back on the Panthers. To make matters worse, with Gerry out of the game, Alec Routledge was brought back to the infield. With him behind the plate, some of the confidence the Panthers had built up during the game began to disappear.

Coach Blackwood called a time out to talk to his team, who seemed to be withering before his very eyes. "Okay, guys," he said, "snap out of it! There's no need to be so discouraged. Haven't you noticed that you've been able to get hits from "Wild Toby" today, and that you were ahead for most of this game? Routledge has been warned not to cause trouble from behind the plate, and I think he'll play it straight after what happened here last time." He glanced over at Tim, who was sitting on the bench looking down at his hands. "Even if he doesn't behave himself, I know you guys are a class act and will be able to keep your focus on the ball where it belongs. Now get out there and finish this game off."

Buzz Baxter was up first, and all his teammates sprang to their feet to cheer for him. All but Tim, that is. Tim just sat on the bench, with his elbows on his knees and his head in his hands.

"What's up, Tim?" Coach Blackwood said, as he sat down beside Tim.

"I just can't get that last game out of my mind, Coach," Tim answered with a sigh. "I was okay with that new guy behind the plate, but now that Alec's back I don't know if I can trust myself. Even in the outfield, he was calling us some pretty vicious names, you know. It really makes me mad."

"So what are you suggesting? Do you think I should pull you from the game? Are you saying you can't handle this?"

"I just don't know. What do you think, Coach?"

Coach Blackwood paused to consider for a moment. "I think I wouldn't have chosen you as my captain if I hadn't trusted your instincts and admired your leadership with the other boys. I think you can go out there and keep your temper under control and maybe even lead us to a victory here. That's what I think."

Tim smiled up at the big, gruff man. "Thanks, Coach," he

said quietly. "That's what I needed to hear. I won't let you down."

"Well, kid, I'm going to have to take you at your word, and right now. You're up."

Tim jumped to his feet and quickly went to select his "lucky bat", the one he'd used twice before today to get hits. But it wasn't there. Where could it have gone? Tim wondered. There was no time to find out, though, because they were waiting for him at the plate. So Tim chose his second favorite, the blue Louisville Slugger, and strode into position. He could see Buzz out on third base, but the two batters between Buzz and Tim in the batting order were out already.

The bat felt weird as he took his warm-up swings, but he stayed focused on the pitcher and the ball. In the fuss over the missing bat, he hadn't even thought about Alec behind the plate, until he heard again that quiet voice, muttering, "Tiny Tim, Timid Tim, Tim the Twit." Tim rolled his eyes in frustration, and tried to get his mind on the ball.

Toby wound up for his first pitch. This pitch was a slider, a pitch that Tim hadn't seen before from Toby. He was totally fooled by it. Strike one.

From behind him Tim heard, "Gotcha! Gotcha! Gotcha!" Alec just kept going with that one annoying word, until the pitch crossed the plate. Tim was rattled, and he swung and missed a pitch that he saw too late was way too high. Strike two.

Tim could feel his anger welling up. He had let himself down by paying attention to what Alec was saying instead of keeping his eye on the ball. He knew that he had let down his teammates, Coach, and his family; but his anger was focused on the red-headed boy right behind him.

He turned to look at him. He could feel that old "urge to kill" rising up inside him. Then suddenly, he could feel his parents watching him and he could hear their words of support after the last game. He reminded himself that "A wise man keeps himself under control". And he could see those disgusting green shirts out of the corner of his eye – all five of them!

Then Tim just laughed. "You can try to get me, Alec," he said with a smirk. "But I've got God on my side, and I choose to be a wise man." Alec was puzzled, but at least he kept quiet during the next pitch.

Tim still felt somewhat off balance with the new bat, but he could see a good pitch coming his way and he knew it was all his. So he swung and he connected. It wasn't the best hit of his career, but it got him safely to first base, and more importantly it got Buzz across the plate for the game-winning run.

And most importantly of all, the Tim Solomon Fan Club really had something to celebrate that night over two large pizzas from Tim's favorite pizza joint, Pizza Heaven. They celebrated the wisdom of a young Solomon, who had learned to look at a frustrating situation with humor rather than anger.

THE PRICE OF FRIENDSHIP
(Proverbs 14:7)

Tryouts for the Col. G.P. Brady Public School boys' volleyball team were over. Satisfied with his efforts, Tim Solomon stuffed his school clothes into his knapsack, deciding to wear his gym clothes home. As he was leaving the change room, he heard a familiar voice call his name. "Tim! Hey, Tim, wait for me."

It was the voice of his new friend, Steve McGrady. Steve had just moved to Parkesville in the summer and had been assigned to Tim's 8th grade class. Their teacher, Mrs. Lassila, had put them both at the same worktable, and their friendship had been growing through the early weeks of September.

Steve and Tim had lots of fun together – sometimes enough to get them in trouble with Mrs. Lassila. Steve had a bizarre sense of humor, and Tim had a hard time resisting his jokes even when he knew he was supposed to be doing schoolwork. Tim usually took his schoolwork seriously. His friend Steve did not, but somehow he did very well on tests and assignments without putting any effort into it.

It turned out that Steve was also good at volleyball – really good. The fact that he was already almost six feet tall didn't hurt. His serves were unreturnable, his spikes were out of everyone's reach, and his miraculous shots all seemed effortless. Tim was impressed. He was pretty sure that he was going to make the team, as he had the year before, but he was absolutely certain that Steve would make the cut.

"Good workout, huh, Tim?" Steve said, when he joined Tim in the corridor outside the change room.

Tim nodded in agreement. "You were awesome!" Tim told

his friend in admiration. "I wish you'd teach me that serve of yours. I can get to it, but I sure can't do anything with it!"

"What?" Steve said, grinning. "Give away my secret weapon? No way!!"

"Ah, c'mon, Steve," Tim begged, "we're going to end up on the same team after all!"

"Good point," Steve answered, slapping Tim playfully on the shoulder. "I guess I could teach you my little trick after all. When do you want your lesson?"

"Why not right now? Can you come home with me? We could practice a bit in the back yard. I'm sure I can find an old volleyball somewhere."

"Sounds good." As he spoke, Steve reached into a deep pocket in his jacket and pulled out a cell phone. He quickly dialed a number, and Tim heard him say, "Carrie. I'll be home late. Yeah, yeah, yeah. Bye."

Tim wondered who Carrie was. But there was something about Steve: he was smart and fun, but you didn't ask him personal questions. Tim had no idea how he knew that, but somehow Steve had made it perfectly clear. Steve was in charge of what topics were talked about and what topics were not; and Tim, if he wanted to be his friend, had better stick to the approved topics.

And Tim knew he wanted to be Steve's friend. First, the Solomon children had been encouraged to befriend new kids, to make them welcome. Second, this guy was cool. Not only was he good at sports and at schoolwork; he was good looking, with his deep tan and black curly hair, and he wore the best clothes–brand name, of course. Steve had a confidence about him that made the other kids feel somewhat intimidated, yet drawn to him at the same time. Tim had been pleased and proud when Steve had selected him out of all the class to pal around with.

"Where to, little buddy?" Steve said, smiling down at Tim, as he folded up his cell phone and put it back into his pocket.

* * *

Tim and Steve found Tim's mom, Julianna Solomon, out in her garden, beginning the fall clean-up. As she saw the boys approaching, she stood up and pushed her hair back, smudging her face with dirt in the process.

"Mom, this is my friend, Steve McGrady," Tim said, carefully leading Steve through Julianna's array of gardening tools.

"Well, hello, Steve," Julianna smiled. "I've been hearing about you since school started, so I'm glad to finally meet you."

"Hello, Mrs. Solomon," Steve answered, flashing a dazzling smile. "It's nice to meet you too. And may I congratulate you on the nice young man you're raising here. Tim, I mean." *Wow!* thought Tim. *Where'd he get a line like that?*

Julianna laughed. "Well, I have a few other nice young people around here too. Have you met Taylor?"

"No, I don't believe I've had the pleasure."

"She's my twin," Tim put in. "She's in the other 8th grade class. She looks a bit like me, except I'm much handsomer."

Steve grinned at his friend, then turned to Julianna. "Well, if Taylor looks anything like you, Mrs. Solomon, I'm sure she's just lovely." Tim winced. *Oh man!* He thought. *Polite is good, but that's a bit much!*

Julianna was self-consciously rubbing at the dirt on her face, but Tim could tell she was pleased by Steve's compliment.

Just then, Peter ran through the yard, kicking a soccer ball, pursued by Emma, who was trying to intercept it. Emma's giggling was getting in the way of her athletic performance. "And now you have met my two other 'lovely' children, Emma and Peter," Julianna said.

"What a nice family you have, Mrs. Solomon," Steve answered, still smiling. Then without missing a beat, Steve continued, "Would you like some help here in the garden, ma'am?"

"No, that's alright, Steve. I'm just about finished with what I'm doing. Anyway, if you help me, I'll have no excuse for staying out here on this beautiful day. But thanks anyway. You two just take care of yourselves."

"Steve is going to teach me his killer serve," Tim explained. "Do you think he could stay for dinner?"

"Sure, if he'd like to and it's okay with his folks."

"Thanks, Mrs. Solomon, I'd like that very much."

As Tim and Steve went to the garage to search for a ball, Tim wondered if Steve would call the mysterious Carrie again.

He did not, nor did he call anyone else.

* * *

When Steve went home after dinner that night, everyone had questions about him. Julianna wanted to know where he had learned such nice manners. Tim's dad, Jake Solomon, wanted to know who his parents were and what they did. Taylor was tongue-tied for once, in shock at having shared a meal with a boy her age who was so tall, dark, and handsome. Emma was interested in where he got his fancy clothes. And Peter, the youngest of the Solomon children and small for his age, wanted to know what he ate to make him grow so tall.

Tim couldn't give any of them the answers they wanted. "I don't know. He's very private. With Steve, you just don't ask."

It was a mystery.

* * *

Both Steve and Tim made the volleyball team, so they spent

more and more time together as the season progressed. Tim's best friend, Ryan Barnicke, often joined them to play 2-on-1 basketball after school, or just to hang out.

It turned out that Steve's favorite place outside of a gym was a shopping mall. Although Tim wasn't too comfortable just "hanging out" at the mall, he didn't want to disappoint Steve. Steve said that what he liked best about the mall was watching the people, but Tim soon had suspicions that there was more to it than that.

One Saturday morning, Tim, Ryan, and Steve had walked together to the Four Points Mall. Tim had a bit of money to spend, but he hadn't decided what he was going to buy. The other boys were broke, so the three happily wandered the mall for an hour or so, trying to spend Tim's money.

As they were passing the food court, Steve pointed to a group of girls about their age.

"Look at that fat one in the orange shirt. Man, she should stay away from the French fries!" He flashed that dazzling grin of his.

Tim nodded and smiled weakly in response, but Ryan shot back, loudly enough to be heard by the girls they were staring at. "Barge coming through!" He burst out laughing and so did Steve.

A bit further down the mall, the boys found themselves slowed in their progress by the crowd of shoppers. Tim and Ryan were in no hurry, but Steve muttered, "I wish these old geezers would move it!" Then he swore and pushed his way through. Tim and Ryan exchanged glances, but followed as quickly as they could manage.

A bit later, they were passing the Bad Weather Shop, a popular young adult clothing store, when Steve stopped them. He struck a pose in front of the store window, and it took just a few seconds for the boys to look past Steve and see the mannequin behind him in the window striking the same pose and wearing exactly the same outfit. They all laughed.

"Hey, Tim," Ryan quipped, "which one's the mannequin and which one is the real Steve McGrady?"

"The real Steve McGrady? He's pretty hard to find." Tim laughed, but as he looked at Steve he realized from his friend's expression that he had crossed into one of Steve's forbidden zones. He had said something he shouldn't have said.

Steve dropped his pose, looked away from the other two boys, and muttered, "Not hard to find, just hard to catch." Or that's what Tim thought he heard.

Tim just couldn't decide what to spend his money on. He was careful with his money, and didn't want to spend money just to spend money. He wasn't sure if he should use the money to buy a few new CDs, or whether he should buy that new white T-shirt he really needed. The CDs would be more fun, but the shirt would be more practical. So Ryan and Steve dutifully followed Tim into one clothing store after another, and into all the CD shops that the Four Points Mall had to offer.

When their tour of the mall was over, Tim had bought nothing but a round of ice cream sundaes at the food court. As they were finishing their ice cream, Steve reached inside his jacket and pulled out a CD, the latest from the Front Yard Boys. Ryan and Tim's eyes were wide.

"Wow!" Ryan shrieked. Ryan liked to be dramatic! "Where'd you get that? That's supposed to be the best!!"

"Oh, didn't you see me pick it up back at Ron the Record Man?" Steve answered.

Tim looked searchingly into Steve's face. "But you said you didn't have any money."

"Yeah, well... I thought I'd surprise you. Somebody's got to keep the economy going. You're not going to do it, if you keep your money in your pocket!" There was that dazzling grin again.

Ryan couldn't contain his excitement. "Let's get out of here!

Where can we go to listen to it? I've been dying to hear this one!"

They headed back to Tim's place to try it out.

* * *

Sundays at the Solomons' were for church and family. The Sunday following their visit to the mall with Steve, Tim invited Ryan back to his house after church. Julianna and Emma were working on lunch, so Tim took Ryan outside to shoot some baskets while they waited. They knew they would be on the lunch clean-up squad.

The score was Ryan 8 – Tim 2. Ryan was happy to be winning, but he noticed that Tim was missing easy shots and not fighting very hard to get the ball.

"What are you thinking about, Tim? Your mind seems to be miles away," Ryan said, deeking around Tim to go in for a lay-up. 10 - 2.

In a burst of new energy, Tim grabbed the ball and dribbled it decisively down the driveway away from his friend. Then he threw a 3-pointer that surprised both of them with its clean entry into the net. 10 - 5.

The boys continued their game for a few minutes, and then Tim said, "Time out, okay? I do have something on my mind."

Ryan took the ball, and the two boys went to sit on the picnic table in the backyard, their feet resting comfortably on the bench below. "So, what gives, Tim Tim?" Ryan liked to tease Tim with the nickname Taylor used since they were kids.

"It's Steve..."

"Yeah, he's cool, huh?"

"Yeah, he's cool, but..." Tim paused to consider his words. He knew how much Ryan admired Steve.

"But what? We had a great time yesterday. We could learn a lot from him."

"That's what I'm afraid of."

"What do you mean?"

"Well, he's a great guy, but he says some things sometimes..."

"Like what? I don't get it."

"Like the swearing for starters."

"Oh, Tim, everybody swears but you and me! Haven't you noticed that?" Ryan jumped down from his spot on the picnic table, and started to dribble the ball back toward the driveway.

"Well, we know better." Tim followed Ryan back to the driveway, and quickly gained possession of the ball. He stopped moving, held the ball tightly across his chest, and faced Ryan.

"Listen, Ry, why haven't we said anything to Steve to get him to stop?"

Ryan was impatient with this whole conversation. He just wanted to play basketball. "Because he'd dump us, that's why. Anyway, what's the big deal? A couple of swear words aren't going to hurt us. Are they?"

"Well, I don't know about you, but now when I'm mad about something or frustrated, I hear Steve's words in my head. And I actually swore out loud yesterday, and all I had done was drop my homework on the floor. That can't be good. My folks would kill me if they heard. And I didn't feel good inside when I did it."

"Oh, come on, Tim, you're getting carried away, aren't you? They're only words."

"Oh, maybe."

"So, can we get back to our game?" Ryan poked the ball, trying unsuccessfully to dislodge it from Tim's grip.

"Well, there's something else. And this concerns you, too, Ry. Did you notice the way Steve was criticizing people. Like that girl at the food court, for example?"

"The girl at the food court?"

70

"Yeah, the big girl. You two made rude remarks about her."

"So, who are you? Mr. Perfect? Anyway, we were just having a bit of fun."

"Fun, Ryan? You were both talking loud enough to really hurt her feelings."

"So? Steve started it!"

"Yeah, but Ryan, you didn't have to pick up on it. That's not you..."

"Who says?" Ryan demanded. This time when he poked the basketball, he made sure that it went flying. "I've had enough of this discussion. I'm outta here!"

"Ryan!" Tim called after his friend, but Ryan just kept on going. Tim, discouraged, squatted against the garage door and put his head in his hands.

He hadn't even got to the part of yesterday's story that *really* bothered him.

* * *

Tim's next visit to the mall took place later that week. He had decided that he couldn't put off buying the white T-shirt after all. Ryan was still mad at him, so Tim asked Steve if he'd like to go along with him after a volleyball practice.

As soon as they were inside the shopping center, Tim regretted asking Steve to come along. It seemed that the more time they spent together, the more critical Steve got of other people, and the more swear words he used. Finally, Tim had to speak up.

"Steve," he said, "I don't mean to criticize, but do you think you have to swear like that all the time?"

Steve's response was swift. "Ah, come on, Tim, don't be such a wimp. You can really be a spoil sport sometimes."

After that, Tim knew better than to mention Steve's rudeness. He knew he'd get nowhere. So he just clammed up and followed Steve down the mall. Soon they had reached their destination, the Bad Weather Shop. Steve's outfit was no longer in the window. Tim stopped outside the store to admire the brand name clothes featured in the new display.

"You stay here, Tim," Steve said quietly, putting his hand firmly on Tim's arm. "I'll take care of this."

"Pardon?" Tim asked, but Steve had already left him standing there.

Steve was back in less than a minute. He was walking quickly and Tim wondered briefly if he had a stomach ache. He was holding his stomach with one hand, as he grabbed Tim and guided him away with the other.

"What's going on?" Tim asked urgently.

"Well, little buddy, I just thought I'd save you some of that money you're so anxious to hang onto." Steve looked over his shoulder a few times, then pushed Tim into the deserted corridor that led to the mall washrooms. He reached inside his jacket, and pulled out a white T-shirt. "I hope it's the right size. You're a medium, right?" Steve flashed him his biggest most charming smile.

"But, Steve... I can't..."

But Steve insisted, "Of course you can! How do you think I get all these great clothes? My old man sure wouldn't get them for me."

Tim was speechless, and when he took the shirt from his friend he had a painful tingling in his fingers.

* * *

"Dad, I'm in a mess," Tim blurted out. He dropped the white T-shirt on the corner of his dad's desk.

Jake took off his glasses, laid them on top of the pile of papers he had been working on and gave his son his full attention. "A mess? What's up?"

"I don't know what to tell you. It's Ryan. And Steve. And now this." Tim was pointing to the T-shirt.

"Now I'm really confused. Why don't we start with the shirt? Looks like a nice enough shirt to me."

"Yes, but it's not mine."

"So, whose is it?"

"Well, nobody's actually. No, it's the store's." Tim was getting more muddled by the second. "It's stolen, Dad." There; it was out.

"What? You stole this shirt?"

"No, Dad, I didn't steal it. Steve did. But he stole it for me. He knew I needed it, but I didn't want to spend the money. So he just made me stand outside the store, and when he came back out he had it under his jacket."

Jake had had some experience through school with kids shoplifting, but he never expected to have to deal with it in his own home, especially not with his level headed first-born son. "So, what did you do when he showed it to you?"

"That's the thing, Dad. I didn't do anything. I can't argue with Steve; I just can't. So I just took the shirt from him and came straight home. I'm a coward, aren't I?"

"Not a coward, son. But you have allowed yourself to be manipulated. And now you're indirectly involved in a crime. You know you have to return the shirt."

"Of course, I do. But how? If I take it to the store, they'll want to know how I got it. I can't rat out a friend."

"Would a real friend get you involved in something like this?"

Tim had to think about that.

"Okay, Tim, here's what we're going to do," Jake began. "You and I will go over to your friend Steve's house and talk to his parents. Then we'll decide what to do from there."

"You know something, Dad? I've never heard Steve talk about his parents. He calls someone named Carrie if he's coming to our place, but he never says much to her. And he never says anything at all about her, or anyone else."

"Well, for better or for worse, we're about to find out more about your friend Steve."

* * *

The man who opened the door to Jake and Tim later that night was very tall and distinguished looking. His slate gray hair was cut short, and he was expensively dressed. "I'm Frank McGrady," he said, shaking hands with Jake. "Won't you come in. My wife will join us when she gets the baby settled." He led Jake and Tim into a beautifully decorated living room. "I'd ask Steve to join us as well," he continued, "but we don't know where he is. He usually shows up around nine."

Tim could tell by his dad's hesitation that Jake was trying to figure out what to make of this man. Tim himself was wondering, *Nine o'clock? And his dad doesn't even mind?*

Tim's thoughts were interrupted by Jake's words: "Steve is a friend of Tim's from school."

"Oh? I didn't know," Mr. McGrady replied. "Steve doesn't tell us too much about his life."

"Yes...well... Today Steve and Tim were at the mall together, and... Well... There's no good way to say this, Mr. McGrady. Steve shoplifted this T-shirt from the Bad Weather store at the Four Points Mall. Tim was planning to buy it, but Steve picked it up and gave it to him instead."

"Yes?" The news had not changed either Mr. McGrady's tone of voice or his perfectly poised manner.

"You don't seem upset, Mr. McGrady."

"Well, I'm afraid it's not the first time it's happened. We thought he had stopped but apparently not. What a nuisance."

There was an awkward pause in the conversation as Jake considered this man and his attitude, so completely unexpected.

"Well, Mr. McGrady, we were hoping that Steve would come with us tomorrow when we return the shirt to the store. I think it would go easier for him if he owned up to it and showed that he was sorry."

"Thank you, Mr. Solomon. You do what you must. I'll take care of it from our end." Mr. McGrady rose from his chair, clearly inviting Jake and Tim to leave. "I'm sorry you didn't get to meet my wife, Carrie. She'll regret having missed you," he said, all polished formality, ushering the Solomons out the front door.

* * *

The next day when Jake and Tim returned to the Bad Weather Shop with the shirt, Jake asked for the manager, a Mr. Corelli. Steve and his dad were nowhere to be seen, but when Mr. Corelli came bustling out to meet them, it was evident that he had been expecting them.

Tim explained how he had come to have the shirt, apologized, and offered to pay for the shirt.

The manager put up his hands and shook his head. "Don't worry, Tim. The shirt has been paid for. It's all been taken care of to the satisfaction of my company by Mr. McGrady." Corelli caught Jake's eye and winked. "He's a hotshot lawyer, you know."

Jake and Tim left the store, relieved that there would be no legal consequences, but unsure of what exactly had happened there.

* * *

Jake took Tim for a donut and a drink at the food court after their interview at the Bad Weather Shop.

"I don't get it, Dad," Tim said, picking up his chocolate dipped donut, but not biting into it.

"I'm not sure I do, either, son. Which part of it don't you get?"

"Steve shoplifts, and his dad doesn't even care. You'd kill me if I did that."

Jake laughed. "Yeah, I probably would. But, you see, your mother and I have tried to teach you children where we stand on things. The McGradys don't share our values. Mr. McGrady thinks the best he can do for his son is to cover up for him."

"The best he can do for himself, don't you think? It couldn't be good for a lawyer to be found to have a son who's a thief, would it?"

"Good point. You're probably right. I try not to judge, but it does look that way."

"I used to like Steve so much, Dad. Now I don't know what to think."

"It's hard, I know. I'll try to give you some insights from the Bible. First, we're meant to love everyone as Christ does. Also, in Proverbs, Solomon has a lot to say about people he calls fools. Those are people who like to hear themselves talk, but who aren't interested in hearing anything from others. They think they're right, and they're not about to change. I'm afraid your friend Steve and his dad are in that category. Solomon's advice for you would be to 'Stay away from a foolish man, for you will not find knowledge on his lips.'"

"Solomon is right, too, Dad."

Jake laughed. "Oh, do tell."

"I never told you this, but I could feel myself changing to please Steve, swearing and stuff. I knew it was wrong but I couldn't stop. He had some kind of power over me."

Jake smiled in approval of Tim's insights.

"So, it seems mean," Tim continued, "but I just have to stop hanging out with him, don't I?"

Jake nodded. "I think that's your best bet. Pray for him and wish him well, but until he changes, steer clear."

Then Jake and Tim dove into their donuts. The whole ordeal had made them really hungry.

"Tim, Mr. Solomon!" They heard Ryan's voice above the voices of the shoppers at the food court. Ryan spotted them waving, and rushed over to join them. "I called your house, Tim, and your mom told me what you were doing. I came over as soon as I could. How did it go?"

"Well, it seems to be all straightened out," Tim answered.

"And Tim is older and wiser!" Jake added.

"Yeah, right," Tim laughed.

"So, listen, Tim, I'm really sorry," Ryan said. "You were right and I was wrong. Can you forgive me?"

"Of course, friend!" Tim was smiling ear to ear.

Jake didn't know what they were talking about, but he didn't ask. He was satisfied with the grin on the face of his young Solomon, who had learned a valuable lesson about fools and about real friendship.

CARD CRAZY
(Proverbs 16: 11)

Seven-year-old Peter Solomon was the youngest of the Solomon family. Sometimes he felt as if his older siblings, twelve-year-old twins Tim and Taylor, and nine-year-old Emma, didn't know he was alive. The family was always running here and there to attend baseball games for Tim, track meets for Taylor, and violin recitals for Emma. But what Peter was interested in, the family just couldn't understand. His passion was collecting SuperSport cards.

SuperSport cards were the latest craze among the younger students at Col. G.P. Brady Elementary School. They were based on the hit TV series "Adventures of SuperSport", which Peter and his friend Bobby Pastorelli watched every day right after school, when they were allowed. They usually watched the show at the Solomons' house, where Bobby went after school when his mom was at work. Today, though, Bobby's mom was home so they had gone to the Pastorellis', next door to the Solomons', to play until show time.

Peter and Bobby were now busy with their other favorite activity: counting, arranging, rearranging, recounting, and talking about their cards. Everyone at home teased the boys about how much time they spent on SuperSport, but Peter and Bobby realized that "old people" just couldn't understand how cool SuperSport was!

Peter had spread his large collection on Bobby's bed. Bobby was holding his smaller deck behind his back as he and Peter admired the brightly colored cards. These cards represented different aspects of most sports played around the world.

"Boy, Peter," Bobby exclaimed, "you sure are lucky! You must have a zillion cards here!"

Peter laughed. "I wish! Actually, I have 124. I had 74 until Grandpa McNab gave me $20 for helping him rake his leaves. I bought five X-packs. 50 new cards! And most of them weren't doubles. I was real lucky."

"Got any you want to trade?"

"Sure!" Peter had no need to check; he knew every card in his collection. "My best traders are Swish, Striker, Goalpost, and Netminder. Have you got any of the Championship Series?"

"Nah, how about you?"

"I have Stanley Cup and World Series. Wanna see?" Peter said. "I keep them hidden in here." He reached into the inside pocket of his knapsack, where he kept his most valuable cards.

Bobby admired the cards. "These holographics are so cool! Which others do ya want?"

"World Series is my favorite. Plus maybe Wimbledon and Masters. I'd give Masters to my grandpa if I got it, 'cos he's always watching golf on the TV. Plus I'd really like Zamboni. That's not Championship Series, but I still think it's real cool."

"I don't have any of those, but wouldya like Puck?"

"Nah, I have it."

"Bogie? Or Laps?"

"Sure! I don't have either of them. Which of my two do you want?"

"I really want Goalpost. He's powerful! And I'll take Swish," Bobby said, continuing to shuffle through his cards. "But let me keep looking. I might have something else in my pile to trade for Netminder. She's pretty cool too."

Peter smiled. He was very proud of his collection, and happy with the trades they had made so far.

Bobby thumbed through his cards for a while, then he looked up at Peter. "Hey, Peter, what do you think of that

Walter guy at school? You know, Walter Swan from the fifth grade?"

"Do you mean the kid with the huge SuperSport collection?" Bobby nodded.

"He's cool. He has an amazing collection, don't you think?"

"Yeah, but...," Bobby said. "I've seen him trade with some of the little kids. He doesn't always trade one for one. Sometimes he talks the Grade Ones into trading three or four of their cards for one of his. He makes up stories about why his cards are so special, and they believe him. That's why he's got so many cards."

"Well, they wouldn't trade if they didn't want to."

"Maybe... But how can they say no to a guy who's so much bigger than they are, and mean too."

Peter thought about that for a second, but then his cards caught his attention. He just had to count them again to be sure how many he had.

Bobby looked at the clock on his bedside table before going back to his own cards. It was 3:57. Only three minutes until "Adventures of SuperSport"! "Hey, Peter, look at the time! Let's go down to the family room for SuperSport!"

He didn't have to ask Peter twice!

* * *

The next day at morning recess, Peter didn't see Bobby or any of his other friends when he got to the playground. Instead he spotted a group of kids with Walter Swan, so he wandered over to see what Walter was up to. Walter was easy to spot because he was so much bigger than the kids he was with, who turned out to be some Kindergartners. Walter was making SuperSport trades. Peter watched Walter in action for a while. Walter would explain to the younger kids how "valuable" or "powerful" or "cool" his cards were, and they would give him two or three or even four of their cards to exchange. Of course, Peter knew that Walter's cards weren't special at all, but the little kids were happy anyway. They were probably pleased just to get attention from a big kid, Peter thought to himself.

Peter looked up and noticed that Bobby had arrived and was also watching the group. Peter could tell from Bobby's face that he wasn't happy, but Bobby didn't say anything – not until he saw Walter include a Monstro card in a trade with a little boy who looked about four years old.

"Hey, Walter," Bobby said, "that's a Monstro card."

Walter looked up at Bobby and smirked. "So?"

"Nobody's traded Monstro since last year. That card is useless, and you know it!"

"So?" Walter's smirk had turned into a glare.

Faced with Walter's angry expression, Bobby stammered, "So...so... that's not fair!"

"So?" Walter didn't have much of a vocabulary. He stood up to face Bobby, his hands on his hips. He was at least five inches taller than Bobby.

Peter was suddenly worried about his friend. "Come on, Bobby, let's go," he said, grabbing Bobby's arm and pulling him toward the school doorway. "This guy's trouble."

But Bobby shook off Peter's hand and faced Walter. "Walter, you shouldn't cheat this little kid."

By this time the kindergarten boy was in tears, and the yard duty teacher was on his way over to see what was happening.

Walter was up and away quickly, but not before he said through his teeth, "Just stay out of my way, Bobby Pastorelli. Or you'll be sorry."

Just then, the bell rang to end recess. Peter and Bobby didn't have a chance to talk about what had happened. By the time school had ended for the day, it seemed to Peter that Bobby had forgotten the nasty incident.

* * *

Peter couldn't stop thinking about what he had seen. He was proud of Bobby for standing up to Walter, and he was a bit worried about what Walter might do to his friend. There were lots of schoolyard rumors about the fights Walter had been in. People said he kicked dogs and stole kids' lunches – that kind of thing.

But Peter couldn't figure out what was wrong with Walter's trades. After all, the kindergarten boy had been happy with the trade until Bobby had interrupted. It wasn't Walter who had made the kid cry; it was Bobby! He sure could see why Walter was happy with the trade, and the little kid was happy too, so where was the harm in it? And, Peter thought to himself, if I traded like that, imagine the collection I would have...

During morning recess the next day, the boys played soccer-baseball against the girls, but at afternoon recess, everyone took out their SuperSport cards. Peter had been thinking about his collection all day. He couldn't help but like the picture in his mind: himself, Peter Solomon, the #1 SuperSport trader of Col. Brady School... Of Parkesville... Of the known universe...!

So when the bell rang for afternoon recess, Peter headed toward the kindergarten door with some of his cards in hand. He saw a girl and a boy holding cards and talking together, and he went right over to them.

"Want to trade?" Peter coaxed.

The little girl's huge smile would have melted his heart under other circumstances, but Peter had one thing on his mind: his SuperSport empire.

Peter recognized the little boy: he was Buzz Baxter's little brother Kevin. Kevin started to lay his cards out on the ground for Peter to see. He shouldn't lay them out, Peter thought, or someone will swipe some.

But before he said anything, Peter spotted *them*. The cards he wanted most in all the world: Wimbledon, Masters, World Cup and – his all-time favorite – Zamboni! Peter was so excited he could hardly keep still! He was pretty sure that Kevin had no idea how good those cards were, because his big brother Buzz wasn't into SuperSport. And Peter wasn't about to explain!

Those four cards together were gold, and Peter was determined to have them for himself! He had learned a few things from watching Walter the day before. He took a deep breath to calm himself down. Then he went into his act.

"Those are nice, Kevin, but they're not nearly as valuable as mine. I'll give you my Slasher here – it's very powerful – but you'll have to give me World Series and Wimbledon to make it an even trade. Same thing for Netminder; I'll trade her for Masters and Zamboni. Those are good trades for you, Kevin. Waddya say?"

"Okay, I guess," Kevin said as he gathered up the four cards and handed them to Peter.

As Peter gave Kevin the two cards they had agreed on, he looked up and saw Bobby, watching the whole thing. Peter caught Bobby's eye. He smiled weakly at his buddy, but Bobby scowled and walked away.

Peter had just made the best deal of his life, so why did he suddenly feel so bad?

* * *

After school, Bobby snubbed Peter and walked home with his older sister Angela. *Bobby and Angela fight all the time*, Peter thought to himself. *Bobby must be awful mad to tag along with her.*

When Peter got home, his mom had a snack waiting for him in the kitchen, as she always did. Bobby had already wolfed his down and gone to watch TV. Peter gave his mom an absent-minded hug and then went straight to his room without touching his cookies and milk. Julianna Solomon watched her youngest son leave the kitchen counter, then she shrugged her shoulders and went back to fixing dinner.

When he got to his room, Peter dropped his knapsack on the chair and flopped down on his bed. There were a million things he could do, lots of toys and activities in his toy cupboard – not to mention homework or the SuperSport show – but Peter couldn't think of anything but little Kevin's excited face as he had taken those two cards from Peter and put them with his pack. Actually, it wasn't the excitement that bothered Peter so much as the trust in Kevin's eyes as he had laid all those cards down for Peter to see, and also when he had accepted Peter's word about the trade.

Peter had the best cards in the SuperSport trading world in his knapsack, and he couldn't even force himself to pull them out and look at them.

He felt rotten inside.

* * *

Peter was still lying on his stomach on his bed when his dad poked his head in to call Peter to supper. "How was your day, bud?"

"Good," Peter muttered.

"How was school?" his dad persisted.

"Good."

"Thanks for all that information!" Jake Solomon said sarcastically. "Oh, I know what you'll tell me about! Did you make any good SuperSport trades today?"

"Nah."

Peter's dad sighed in frustration. Sometimes it was impossible to get his youngest son to talk. "Well, anyway, Pete, it's time to wash up for supper. It's that tuna pasta that you like."

"Okay, Dad," Peter said. "I'll be there in a minute."

Jake was concerned when Peter, who was usually the first to sit down for every meal, didn't budge from his position on his bed.

* * *

The next morning at eight, Bobby was at the Solomons' kitchen door as usual. Bobby and Peter always called for each other for the five-block walk to school, but somehow Peter thought that Bobby wouldn't show that day. When he did, Peter didn't know what to say to his friend as he put on his jacket and stuffed his lunch and homework into his knapsack.

The truth was, Peter hadn't slept very well the night before. He had worried about Bobby being mad at him, and about Walter being mad at Bobby. He had worried about his new cards. He had worried about how he would act and what he would say if he saw Kevin Baxter – or even Buzz Baxter – at school. He had worried about letting Bobby down and disappointing his parents somehow.

The trouble was, he still wasn't sure what was the problem with trades that both kids were happy with. He knew he needed to talk to God about it, but he was afraid to. Why? Because he *really* wanted to keep those four cards for himself.

With all those thoughts chasing each other around in his head, it's no wonder he was tired and confused that day! And Bobby didn't help his mood any...

"That was bad what you did yesterday," Bobby said as soon as they were safely outside the Solomons' house. "You should'na taken those cards from poor Kevin. You're as bad as Walter."

"I didn't try to trade off old useless cards, did I? And I didn't trade him three to one like Walter does, did I? And he was happy with the two cards he got, wasn't he? I'm not like Walter at all." Peter tried to sound sure of himself, but he was having trouble believing his own words.

"You lied, just like Walter does."

Peter couldn't really deny it, but he tried. "Not exactly. Those were both good cards. They just weren't as good as I said they were."

Bobby just stared at Peter, not knowing what to say. Then he spit it out: "I don't like you anymore, Peter Solomon. You tell lies and you're mean to little kids and I don't trust you. Go and see if Walter Swan wants to be your new friend." Bobby wiped a tear from his eye before he ran as fast as he could away from Peter.

Peter's walk to school that day was slow and lonely.

* * *

As Peter turned the corner next to the schoolyard, he heard a huge racket out by the "battle tree". The "battle tree" was an old oak way out in the far end of the schoolyard, as far away as you could get from the school and the teachers, and still be on school property. Because it was usually out of range for the yard duty teacher, big kids often went there if there was something they needed to fight out. Peter had never been involved in any fights at the "battle tree", and he and his friends were usually too scared to go near there. They didn't want to get in trouble with the teachers or with the big kids.

I wonder who it is this time, wondered Peter, as he glanced toward the noise of kids screaming and fighters scuffling on the ground. He was horrified to see that the kid on the bottom of this scuffle was his ex-friend Bobby Pastorelli. And Walter Swan was straddling Bobby, pinning him down. Bobby was struggling bravely, but Walter was landing lots of punches on Bobby's shoulders and his face. Peter could see that Bobby was getting hurt. Walter was so much bigger and stronger than

87

Bobby, not to mention that he had much more fighting experience!

Peter didn't stop to think. If he had, he might not have done what he did. He just ran as quickly as he could to the closest break in the fence and out to the "battle tree". Not caring that he was much smaller and younger than the 5th and 6th graders who had gathered for the "show", Peter elbowed his way through the crowd. All he cared about was getting to Bobby so he could help him out.

A couple of kids from Walter's gang were at the front of the circle around the fighters. When they saw Peter shoving through, they grabbed his arms to hold him back.

"Let the wimp fight his own battles," one of them snarled.

"But Walter's too big, and Bobby's my friend," Peter shouted as he struggled out of their grip.

Suddenly, Peter found himself in the center of the circle of screaming kids, wondering how he had got there. Then he looked down at Bobby and saw blood streaming from a cut on Bobby's mouth and he knew what he had to do.

Peter launched himself onto Walter Swan's shoulders, caught the bully around the neck, and forced him to loosen his hold on Bobby. As Walter fell over with Peter hanging onto his neck, Bobby rolled out from underneath them. Bobby slowly got to his feet and watched Walter and Peter struggling for a moment, looking for his opening. Just as he was about to get back into the fight, they all heard a piercing whistle and the angry voice of Ms. Shaw, the principal.

"Everyone, clear the area! Back to your classrooms! Walter, Peter, Bobby, I'll see you in my office RIGHT NOW!"

Peter looked up from the ground into the shocked face of his big brother, Tim.

* * *

Peter felt numb as he sat between Bobby and Walter in Ms. Shaw's office. He had never been in there before except the time he had helped read the announcements over the P.A. in the morning. His mom and dad had been there, and he had been really proud because he had got it all right.

Peter didn't feel proud now, though.

All three boys were dirty and bleeding, but Bobby had got the worst of it by far. The school nurse had already been by to clean the many scrapes on his face, and you could see that he had a black eye coming. Walter's knuckles were bloody. Peter's knees were a mess, and he felt stiff and sore from rolling on the ground with Walter on top of him.

Ms. Shaw was not sympathetic about their injuries, not at all. She was sitting across the desk from them. Her eyes pierced right through the boys over the tops of her glasses, which were perched on the end of her nose. No one in the whole school ever wanted to be on the bad side of Ms. Shaw, although Walter didn't look as if he cared too much. Walter stared out the window and drummed his fingers on the arm of his chair as she spoke. Was he listening at all? Peter wondered. Then Peter realized, Walter had obviously heard lots of lectures from Ms. Shaw before.

"Walter, since this is the third time this year that you have been involved in a fight on school property, I have no choice but to call your parents and suspend you from school for three days. You will be asked to complete the homework assignments that Mrs. Harvey sends home, and you will come back here to see me, with your parents, on Thursday morning. Now go and collect your things, Walter, and then sit on one of the chairs outside the office until someone comes to get you."

Peter and Bobby solemnly watched Walter leave the office, wondering what Ms. Shaw had planned for them. They were frightened and ashamed, and they had no idea what was in store for them. They sat quietly, heads down, hardly daring to breathe.

"Peter, Bobby, look at me." They looked up and met Ms. Shaw's gaze. Her eyes had lost that scary piercing quality, and looked almost kind. Almost.

"Boys, I'm surprised that two nice boys like you could have got yourself involved in something like this. I am disappointed, but not nearly as disappointed as your parents are going to be when I call them and explain what I saw. My advice to you is that you tell them the whole story when you get home. Beginning to end. Don't try to hide anything."

Peter and Bobby nodded.

"I am not going to send you home today because you have never done anything like this before. I will be calling your parents right now, and you will not be able to go to class for two days. No recesses either. Instead you will work here at the office, and I will be certain that Mrs. Sharkey sends down plenty of extra work to keep you busy. Now, go and sit outside my office until recess – and stay out of Walter's way!"

* * *

If Peter thought sitting in Ms. Shaw's office was tough, it was nothing compared to sitting at the kitchen table across from his mom and dad. He had never seen them so angry, not even the time he had thrown the cat down the stairs.

"There has never been a Solomon sent to the principal's office before, and I was hoping to keep it that way," Peter's dad was saying. "Between Ms. Shaw and Tim, we have quite a good picture of what happened. What came over you? Are you crazy? Fighting on school property? Fighting anywhere is just not okay, young man, and you know it!"

"But, Dad–"

"No 'buts' about it, Peter!" Jake Solomon was livid.

90

"You know it's wrong to fight, Peter. So why did you do it?" Peter's mom asked.

"Well, what was I supposed to do? I came around the corner at school and there was Bobby stuck under Walter. Walter was punching him like crazy. I had to help him."

"And the only way you could think of to help him was to get in there with your fists swinging?" his dad asked.

"That's all I could think of. I just didn't want Bobby to get hurt."

"Wasn't there a teacher around?"

"I dunno. I didn't look. I guess I should have, maybe."

"Maybe?"

"Yeah, I should have."

"You got that right, kid."

Julianna nodded in agreement. "So what was the fight about anyway?" she wanted to know.

"SuperSport cards."

"Don't tell me! How could those cards cause a fight?"

"Bobby tried to stop Walter from cheating some little kids yesterday. Walter was mad."

"I've got to hand it to you two, then," Jake said. "I admire your courage. Bobby was brave to stand up to a boy who is so much older, and you, my son, showed courage in defending your friend when the odds were against you. I'm proud of you for that." Jake reached out and patted Peter's shoulder. "But that's not to say that I ever want to hear about you fighting again. I do not. Agreed?"

"Agreed." Peter smiled, and he and his dad shared a "high five".

But they weren't finished yet. Julianna still had some questions.

"Pete, I'm glad to see you and Bobby are friends again. You were mad at each other yesterday. What was that all about?"

Peter's smile disappeared. Then he remembered Ms. Shaw's

advice to tell his parents the whole story, beginning to end, so he took a deep breath and started his tale, hoping for the best.

"Well, Bobby thought I was trading like Walter..."

"What?" both his parents said together.

Bit by bit, Peter told his story. His card collection. How kids at school admired big traders. How easy Walter made it look to get extra cards. How happy the little kids are to trade with big kids. How Bobby knew it was wrong, and spoke out against Walter right in front of everyone on the playground. How Kevin Baxter had the four best cards in the world. How much Peter wanted those four cards. How bad he had felt afterward.

The story had tumbled out, and Peter felt much better once he had made his confession. His parents listened stony-faced as he talked, smiling only when he reached the end of his story.

"But here's what I don't get. I can see that I did wrong, or I wouldn't have ended up in the office. But I don't get what's wrong with what I did. I got four cards I wanted, and Kevin, the guy I traded with, was so happy."

Julianna was thoughtful. "I think you know in your heart that you were taking advantage of someone younger. Remember how you feel when Tim tells you those stories of his and tricks you into believing they're true. Same thing, only worse, because there was no sense of humor or love attached in your trading. Also, you've helped me understand better one of Solomon's proverbs: 'Honest scales and balances are from the Lord.' You see, God wants honesty in trades and business. And that includes SuperSport cards!"

"And you know that bad feeling you had after you cheated that boy yesterday?" Jake interjected. "That was the Holy Spirit trying to guide you to do the right thing. Sometimes, though, what we want just seems so real to us that we ignore the Holy Spirit. Sad, but very human."

Peter thought about what his parents were saying. "I didn't

even pray about it, because I knew God would want me to give those cards back."

"And does he?" his mom asked.

"Yup. I'll do it first thing tomorrow. I think I'll give Kevin a few extras from my pack as well. He's a good kid, and I was mean to him. I hope he'll forgive me."

"You know, God already has."

* * *

The next morning on the way to school, Peter and Bobby compared notes on how their parents had taken "the News".

"Well, my mom has grounded me for the rest of my life," said Bobby, laughing. "She does that whenever she's really mad at me. It usually lasts a week or so. But I have to miss Cubs and basketball. I hate that! What happened to you?"

"I'm grounded, too. Two weeks. But guess what? My dad said we were both brave. Whaddya think of that? Cool, eh?"

"Brave. Wow. Let's not be brave again for awhile though, okay?"

Peter laughed. "I know what you mean!"

The two boys walked half a block before Peter spoke again.

"I sure am glad we're friends again, Bobby. You were right and I was dumb."

"You were dumb alright, Peter. But you're the best!" Bobby said, and the two exchanged their private handshake: a left-handed shake, two slaps and a rub.

The two boys were grinning as they walked along.

"So," Bobby said, "want to go to Mark's Mart after school to see if the next series of SuperSport cards are in?"

"Can't. I'm grounded from SuperSport for two weeks too."

They did go to Mark's Mart, though, to buy their favorite ice cream treats, mint chocsicles. And on the way home, Peter and

Bobby celebrated the wisdom of the youngest Solomon, who had learned about fairness and the importance of friendship.

FRACTURED FRIENDSHIPS
(Proverbs 12: 26, 17: 9)

Vanessa Jones-Fitzgerald lived right around the corner from the Solomons, but every time Taylor Solomon went there to visit Vanessa, Taylor thought she had entered a different world. From the outside, the Jones-Fitzgerald house looked similar to the Solomons' own two-story white house, but inside... Inside was a different matter altogether.

For starters, absolutely everything matched! The whole house – at least the parts Taylor had been to – was decorated in shades of blue and yellow, walls, furniture, and what Taylor thought of as "knicky-knackies", those fancy useless things people have in their home as decorations.

It was beautiful, just like in a magazine; but it was so perfect that Taylor was always afraid she'd make a mistake by moving something or, worse, spilling something. She was always relieved when it was time to go home. It wasn't that she didn't like Vanessa's parents. They were nice and all, when they were home. But the house felt cold and empty compared to the comfortable chaos at the Solomons'.

Taylor never mentioned this to Vanessa, of course. Taylor and Vanessa had been friends since she and her twin brother Tim had met Vanessa on a trip to the neighborhood park as pre-schoolers. At that time, both Taylor and Tim had been enchanted by the fact that Vanessa owned every toy ever advertised on television, and they were more than happy to befriend her. The girls had been almost inseparable ever since.

Vanessa had had a nanny then, because both her parents were away from home so much for their jobs. The nanny's name was Giselle, and she just loved Vanessa; Taylor could tell by the way she got Vanessa's parents to buy Vanessa anything she wanted. (At least, that's how Taylor had seen it then, when she was just four years old. Now that she was thirteen, she was beginning to see things differently.)

Taylor remembered that, even at age four, she had thought it was weird the way Vanessa had ordered Giselle around, but Giselle didn't seem to mind. And what did Taylor know about these things? The Solomons didn't have a nanny; they just had two parents who ran the place!

It was not Giselle who opened the door this time, though; it was Vanessa herself. The Jones-Fitzgeralds had decided that when Vanessa turned thirteen, she didn't need someone to take care of her anymore, and Giselle had gone to work for another family. Taylor missed her, and although she wouldn't admit it, Taylor was sure Vanessa did too.

But for now, Vanessa was enjoying her freedom and independence. Her parents both had important jobs downtown and were seldom home before 8 o'clock, so Vanessa had the run of the place.

When Vanessa opened the door, she was met by Taylor and their new friend, Sara Spencer. Vanessa had bags of chips in both hands. "Hey Tay, Sara," Vanessa said as she opened the door, "come on in. I was wondering when you two would get here. I've just been looking through the kitchen cupboards to see if there's a halfway decent snack, and I can only find these three kinds of potato chips, some cookies, and microwave popcorn. There's soda in the fridge. Do you feel like having anything?"

Sara had been hanging out with Taylor at school and at church ever since she had helped on the carnival committee in the spring. Vanessa went to a private school and did not go to church. But it was inevitable that Sara and Vanessa would meet through Taylor; and Taylor, Vanessa, and Sara had slowly but surely become good friends. Taylor's mom called them the "three musketeers". Jake, Taylor's dad, called Taylor's friends "the long and the short of it", referring to the vast difference in their heights. Vanessa was tiny, barely five feet tall, while Sara was already 5 foot 10 inches and seemed to be in the middle of a growth spurt. Taylor was in the middle of this friendship in more ways than one!

Sara knew Vanessa well, but she had never been to Vanessa's house before. Taylor had planned to warn her ahead of time that the place was a palace, but they had been talking about some outrageous things that had happened at school that day and she had forgotten. At first, Taylor had to force back a giggle as she noticed Sara's reaction to Vanessa's perfect house: her eyes went wide and her mouth fell open. Sara was usually quiet, but now she was tongue-tied! Taylor was disturbed by Sara's reaction as well: she expected some kind of wisecrack from her fun-loving new friend, but Sara's expression had no fun in it. Sara's face showed anger and resentment.

Taylor tried to ease the moment. "So, what do you think of the old barn Nessa lives in, Sara?" she quipped.

"Not bad," Sara replied, "if you're made of money." She tried to smile, but Taylor couldn't help but notice her hesitation.

"So, are you coming in or not? Do you want something to eat?" Vanessa prompted. "I've got everything set up in the music room, if you're not hungry. I thought we could listen to some DVDs while we work on our beads. Good idea? And I want to tell you what happened today at Wellington Castle." Vanessa was a day student at Wellington Castle Ladies College, a prestigious girls' private school in Parkesville.

"Food first, right, Sara?" suggested Taylor. Sara nodded, and they followed their hostess to the kitchen.

The kitchen counters were strewn with bags of chips, cookies, you name it – it was a kids' after-school fantasy! "Pick what you'd like," Vanessa was saying as she headed for the fridge. "Cola? Orange? Grape? Cream soda? Juice? What's your pleasure?"

"You have cream soda? Wow! That's for me!" said Taylor. "My mom won't buy that stuff, except Christmas and Easter. Too much sugar, she says."

Sara seemed unable to make a choice. She just kept looking into the refrigerator, still speechless. Vanessa was getting a bit impatient. "What'll it be, Sara Girl?"

"Cola, I guess," Sara finally whispered.

"You'd think she'd never seen soda before!" Vanessa joked. She reached for a cola can, and tossed it to Sara. "Catch!"

The girls rummaged through the snack bags and chose what they'd like to eat, and then they gathered up their snacks and went off in search of the music room.

The music room was, of course, exquisitely decorated, and contained top of the line sound equipment. Vanessa chose a Front Yard Boys DVD and put it on, and the girls settled down on the floor around the glass coffee table where Vanessa had placed boxes and boxes of multi-colored beads, and the wires and clippers they needed for their favorite hobby, jewelry making. The thick pale blue carpet was comfortable to sit on, and they leaned up against the dark blue leather furniture.

It took awhile before Sara seemed to be herself. She couldn't stop looking around, and she kept rubbing her hand over the soft leather of the armchair that she was leaning on. Vanessa talked away, not appearing to notice anything out of the ordinary. She wanted to share her news about the Christmas Dance they were planning at Wellington Castle; and once Vanessa started talking, it was sometimes hard to get a word in.

Taylor and Sara settled in to a familiar pattern, working steadily on their beadwork while Vanessa entertained them with her chatter. Taylor was working on some bracelets for her sister Emma's Christmas present, and Sara was working on earrings for one of her sisters. She said she'd see how they turned out and then decide who they'd look best on. Sara had three younger sisters, as well as three brothers, so there were lots of possibilities.

The three girls passed the afternoon companionably, sharing design ideas and stories from their schools. Then Sara and Taylor went off to their own homes for supper, as Vanessa waited for her parents to come home.

* * *

A few days later, Vanessa came over to the Solomons' to call for Taylor. Again, the activity of choice was beading, and they went upstairs together to work in the bedroom Taylor shared with Emma. The ET Room, as Tim called it, was a wonderful mixture of color and fabric and posters. The wall on Emma's side of the room was bright yellow and displayed posters of dancers and musicians. The wall on Taylor's side of the room was a vibrant red, and she had hung up team pennants and posters of her favorite athletes. She also had a small plaque that said "Dare to Share" with a picture of Jesus on it. Taylor wanted to be a missionary and was inspired by the challenge of that plaque. The two walls in "neutral territory" were not neutral in color: one was a bright apple green and the other was a warm medium blue. Their curtains and bedspreads were in blocks of all the colors on their walls. The result was shocking but fun, and the girls loved their room. As Vanessa made herself at home there, though, it occurred to Taylor that Mrs. Jones-Fitzgerald would not have allowed such a room in her perfect house.

Vanessa had brought her beading supplies with her, but she made no move to set them out. Instead, she collapsed on her stomach on Emma's bed and blurted out, "Can you believe that Sara?"

Taylor was surprised at her words and at her tone. "What do you mean?" she wondered.

"You didn't notice that she was too stuck up for words the other day at my house?" Vanessa answered. "She wolfed down a whole bag of sour cream and onion chips and two colas, plus she used some of my best beads, but she hardly said two words. What was that about? So rude."

Vanessa looked to Taylor for some kind of agreement, but Taylor only shrugged.

"You mean," Vanessa went on, "you didn't notice how ignorant she was. She must be mad at me or something. Did she say something to you on your way home? You go part way with her, don't you? She must have said something. What did she say?"

Taylor thought about the short walk back to her house that evening. Sara had walked with her and then gone on to her own house, which was in the part of town on the other side of the school. "I dunno, Nessa. Mostly we joked about who did the best beads. We talked a bit about the church pageant coming up. Nothing special. Nothing about you."

"Well, I don't know how you could miss it, Tay. She acted like she was the Queen of England, just sitting there, doing her beads and not saying anything to us peasants. And you know what? I saw her the other day with Frannie O'Brien, giggling and laughing. When I went by them, Sara looked up but she didn't even say hello. I think Miss Spencer thinks she's just too good for us. She just used you, Taylor, to get to know some people when she was new in town, and now she's decided we're not good enough for her. Yup, that's what I think. I'm not going to talk to her anymore. She can be a snob all she wants; I won't even notice!"

"No way, Nessa. I think you've got it all wrong." Taylor was confused by what Vanessa was saying. "I admit she was quieter than usual, but maybe she was just having a bad day."

"Oh, Taylor, you're so naive sometimes," Vanessa insisted. "You just watch. She'll be spreading stories about us before you know it. It happens all the time at Wellington Castle."

"But it doesn't happen to us, Nessa," Taylor said meekly, trying to believe what she was saying.

* * *

Taylor and Vanessa had had a pretty good time at Taylor's that day, but the conversation about Sara kept playing over and over in Taylor's head. She couldn't believe that Sara would just dump her after all the fun they'd had and the secrets they'd shared. But maybe Vanessa was right. Taylor knew that Vanessa was a bit more "mature" than she was, more experienced, more worldly. Taylor thought it came of living with only adults and going to a private school.

Taylor was in her room trying to do her homework, but she felt so unsettled about Sara that she couldn't concentrate. Somehow algebra didn't seem important in the face of a fading friendship. So Taylor went out to the hallway to make a phone call. "Hello, Mrs. Spencer, is Sara there please?" she asked politely.

Mrs. Spencer's answer confirmed her worst fears. "Sorry, Taylor, but she's just gone out for a walk with Frannie. Shall I have her call you back?"

Taylor gasped. "I guess so. If she wants to...," she said, and hung up the phone with a sinking heart.

The evening wore on. Taylor rushed to the phone every time it rang, but the calls were mostly for Tim or her mother. Where was Sara? Why wasn't she calling? Could Vanessa be right after all?

Algebra was out of the question. Taylor moved on to her language arts assignment, but she didn't do very well at that either. The story she wrote was boring, boring, boring.

Sara still hadn't called by the time Taylor went to bed. Taylor's last waking thought was, *What is the matter?*

* * *

Taylor didn't see Sara the next day at school until lunch. She was in the other eighth grade class with Tim. Taylor saved a seat for Sara in the lunchroom, as she did whenever she was eating lunch at school. Today, though, Sara didn't even look for her. She came into the lunchroom with Frannie, and the two of them went straight to a table at the opposite side of the room from where Sara and Taylor usually ate.

Well, Taylor thought, as she ate a tuna fish sandwich that now tasted like dust, *I guess I can't deny it anymore. I've been dumped. Nessa was right. Okay, Sara, two can play at that game.* Taylor looked around her wildly until she saw Caroline McFee enter the lunchroom. Caroline was in Taylor's class. They weren't particularly good friends, but they had worked on a few projects together. Caroline was looking around for a place to sit, and Taylor waved. "Yo, Caroline. There's a seat here."

Pretty soon, Taylor and Caroline were laughing and carrying on. Taylor was pretending to have fun, but all the while she was watching Sara out of the corner of her eye.

* * *

Taylor rushed straight to Vanessa's house that night after school. "You were right," she said to Vanessa even before she had taken off her jacket. "We've been dumped."

"Oh yeah? What happened?"

Taylor told Vanessa about the scene in the lunchroom, and also about the fact that she hadn't seen Sara at recess, either. The whole story made Taylor sad all over again. She still couldn't really believe that a girl she had shared secrets with, even really important secrets about her missionary dreams, had decided to end their friendship.

Vanessa, on the other hand, seemed jubilant at the news. "I knew it! Well, who needs her? We have each other, right? I never liked her anyway. It was better when it was just the two of us, and now it's just the two of us again." That seemed to put the situation to rest for Vanessa, and she led Taylor to the kitchen for one of her renowned after-school snacks.

But Taylor was not happy. Her parents had always taught her that a friend is a friend, not a throw-away commodity. And she was pretty sure Sara had been taught the same thing.

* * *

Saturday morning was unusually quiet in the Solomon household. Only Tim had a game to be chauffeured to, a basketball tournament at the school, and Jake had taken him to it. The younger kids were playing together – wonder of wonders! – happily in the family room.

Taylor was in her room, trying to read <u>The Lion, The Witch, and The Wardrobe</u> for the umpteenth time. It was her absolute favorite book, and she was hoping it would take her mind off her bad mood, the bad mood she hadn't been able to get rid of ever since her realization that Sara was no longer her friend.

Taylor heard a rap at her door. "Come on in," she called gloomily.

It was her mom. "Hey, Taylor, what're you doing?" Julianna asked.

Taylor held up her book in answer.

"It's not often I catch you just lying on your bed with a book. Are you feeling alright?" Julianna sat down at the foot of Taylor's bed, leaned over, and pretended to take Taylor's temperature.

"Yeah, Mom, I'm fine," Taylor answered smiling, but shaking her head to avoid her mom's touch. "I just don't feel like doing anything right now."

"It's a gorgeous day," Julianna prodded. "Why don't you call a meeting of the three musketeers and do something outside?"

"The three musketeers?" Taylor muttered. "More like the two musketeers."

"Two musketeers?" Julianna queried. "Come to think of it, I haven't seen Sara around here in awhile. You two haven't had a fight, have you?"

It was impossible for Julianna to miss the look of sadness and confusion on her daughter's face. "Not a fight, exactly. But Sara doesn't seem to want to hang out with us anymore. I don't know why but she's been avoiding me for a week, ever since we had a meeting at Nessa's house."

"Have you called her?" Julianna asked.

"I did once," replied Taylor, "but she was out with Frannie, and she didn't even bother to call me back!"

"Have you looked for her at school?"

"Yes, of course," Taylor said, exasperated, "but she's always with Frannie. Nessa says we've been dumped. She says Sara just used me to get settled into Parkesville."

"You agree with Vanessa, then?" Julianna wondered.

Taylor shook her head at first, then said, "I don't know what to believe, Mom."

"Well, it doesn't sound like Sara to me," Julianna suggested. "Do you think you might be over-reacting? Is it such a crime for her to spend time with another girl?"

"No, I guess not, but it still hurts. I used to be able to count on her."

"Can I tell you Solomon's take on friendship, honey?" Julianna was smiling encouragingly.

"Is there anything that can stop you, once you've got old

Solly in mind?" Taylor joked. Julianna's love of the Solomon writings in the Bible was well known and was a bit of a family in-joke. Julianna even claimed that she had married Jake because she liked his last name!

"Probably not," Julianna laughed. "Two proverbs come to mind: 'A righteous man is cautious in friendship' and ' He who covers over an offense promotes love, but whoever repeats the matter separates close friends.' What do you think of the first one?"

"'Cautious in friendship'? I don't really know. Cautious is careful, right?"

"Basically. I'm thinking that for your situation it suggests that you should be cautious about how you interpret Sara's actions, and be careful not to act without thinking it through. You wouldn't want to lose a friend over a misunderstanding, would you?"

"Well, no. I miss Sara. I don't want to lose her as a friend," Taylor insisted. "So what do I do?"

"That's where the second proverb comes in. I think you need to start by 'covering over the offense'. Sara has hurt your feelings, but knowing Sara the way we both do, I don't believe that she meant to. Are you prepared to forgive her, to allow your friendship to continue and grow?"

"It's hard, Mom," Taylor admitted. "She's basically snubbed me for an entire week. The worst is at recess and lunchtime. Who am I supposed to hang out with, eat with? I know lots of kids, but no one like Sara. But you're right. Rise above: isn't that what you're always telling us?"

Julianna pressed on. "Now, what about the end of that proverb? 'Whoever repeats the matter separates close friends.'"

"You know Nessa. All she wants to talk about now is Sara, and how she has dumped us and stabbed us in the back. I love Nessa, but it's like she expects the worst of people. She almost makes a game of it." Taylor was silent for a moment as she rifled through the pages of her book. Then she continued, "Now that I think about it, I probably wouldn't have thought that there was trouble between Sara and me if I hadn't let Nessa talk me into it."

"Brilliant deduction, my dear Watson. My good friend Solomon was wise, and so, my darling daughter, are you!"

"So, Mom, I've always wanted to ask you..." ventured the darling daughter, "How *do* you come up with those proverbs...?"

* * *

The next day, Taylor made up her mind to find a way to talk to Sara, no matter what. She even got Coach Briden to excuse her from a basketball practice so she could meet Sara as she left the school. She'd track her down if she had to!

As it turned out, tracking wasn't necessary. Taylor was hanging around the door Sara had to use to get outside from her classroom, and her face lit up when she saw Taylor there.

"Hey, Taylor!" she greeted. "How have you been? I haven't seen you in ages."

"Yeah, I know," Taylor replied. "We don't seem to have been crossing paths very much this week. Where are you off to now?"

"I was just heading home," Sara answered. "I wonder..." Sara was clearly trying to make a decision of some kind. Taylor waited, relieved that Sara was being so friendly, yet curious about what Sara was puzzling over. "How would you like to come home with me for a change? I know my mom would be glad to have you, and I'd love a chance to catch up a bit. I've been working so hard on a project with Frannie O'Brien that I feel like I haven't done anything but schoolwork in ages!"

A project with Frannie O'Brien, Taylor gulped and was suddenly ashamed of herself. No wonder they had had their heads together so intently all these days. Taylor felt so guilty she almost didn't feel right about accepting Sara's invitation. But she was dying to talk to Sara and knew she couldn't miss this chance. "That would be great, Sara! Remind me to call my mom when we get there. We'll be gabbing so much, I might forget."

The two girls laughed and headed off in the direction of Sara's house, gabbing all the while.

* * *

It was several blocks to Sara's house, and they had to walk toward the city center instead of toward the subdivision of newer houses where the Solomons and the Jones-Fitzgeralds lived. Taylor had never been to Sara's house before. As they continued their walk, she realized that she had never been in this part of town before, although she had lived in Parkesville all her life. Sara's house was one of about ten tiny houses on a small dead end street, situated just behind a rundown factory building. As Taylor and Sara turned into a lane way leading to the side door of one of the houses, Taylor found herself wondering, *How can Sara's whole family fit in this house?*

Taylor had met Mrs. Spencer at church, and she recognized her voice calling merrily, "Sara Elizabeth, is that you, darlin'?"

"Yes, Mama," Sara shouted back. "And I've brought Taylor home today. I hope that's okay."

Sara and Taylor were taking off their coats and hanging them on hooks just inside the side door. There were three steps to another door that led into the Spencer home. At the news of Taylor's presence, Taylor sensed a bit of commotion up those stairs, and sure enough, as she came through the door into the Spencers' kitchen, there was Mrs. Spencer scurrying over with her arms wide. "Taylor Solomon, what a treat to see you!"

Taylor would have said something back, but she was pretty

much smothered in Mrs. Spencer's hug. When she could breathe again, Taylor laughed. "Wow! What a welcome! Thanks, Mrs. S."

Once inside Sara's home, Taylor could see that it was dominated by a large kitchen. Amanda and Philip, the two youngest Spencers at three and two, were in booster chairs at the kitchen table, enjoying a snack, and Taylor could hear the sounds of various Spencer siblings coming from three other rooms, all of which opened onto the kitchen. Taylor could see that what had originally been the living room had been made over into a bedroom for Sara's younger sisters Amber and Amanda. Brian and Adam shared another room and for now Philip, the youngest, still bunked in with his parents on a small borrowed cot. These three bedrooms plus the kitchen made up the main floor of the Spencers' house.

So the Spencers lived in and around the kitchen. Mrs. Spencer tried to have a conversation with Sara and Taylor, but it was hard to complete a sentence without one of the other kids either throwing out a wisecrack or interrupting with some irrelevant and silly comment. Laughter was abundant. Taylor was having so much fun she almost forgot to call her mother to tell her where she was.

When there was a short break in the craziness around the Spencer kitchen table, Sara suggested she and Taylor go upstairs for a bit of privacy. "Want to come up and see my room? We call it the Garret. Eloise and I live up there."

Sara led Taylor to a doorway which opened on a set of stairs that were both narrow and steep. The girls climbed the stairs carefully, and soon emerged in a small room with slanted ceilings. Sara and Eloise's room was about half the size of the room Taylor and Emma shared, and you could tell that decorating was not high on the Spencers' list of priorities. There was faded wallpaper on the walls, and the tile floor was covered almost completely by the furniture, a double bed that both girls slept in, a large dresser, and a small table that Sara was using as a desk. The furniture and the bedding looked "well-used", but the whole effect was of warm confusion.

"So, I guess you know now why I've never invited you here before," Sara said hesitantly.

"What do you mean?" asked Taylor. Taylor's immediate reaction to Sara's whole house was that it was very tiny, but she didn't want to say anything to hurt Sara's feelings.

"Well, I don't exactly live in the Taj Mahal, do I?" There was a tinge of bitterness creeping into Sara's voice.

"And I'm glad you don't. How would I ever get to visit you way over in India?"

Sara laughed, but Taylor could see that she was still uncomfortable.

"Can you see now why I was kind of a mess at Nessa's last week? I can't even imagine living like Nessa does! I just couldn't relax because I kept wondering how Nessa would react if I brought her here. We have always had food and clothes and whatever we need for school, but we have never had a soda in our fridge, let alone several kinds at once. And imagine having that whole house to herself! I can't. I don't have a room to myself, let alone a house."

Just then, they could hear footsteps on the stairs to the Garret. It was Eloise coming up to get a sweater. "See what I mean?" Sara said. That touch of bitterness in her voice had returned.

"I had no idea," Taylor said guiltily. "I guess I figured everyone lives like we do. I mean, we're a long way from rich, but we do take a lot of stuff for granted."

"Not me." Sara was shaking her head. "Stuff is for other folks."

"It is fun here, though, you have to admit that! My sides hurt from laughing downstairs!"

"Yeah, I s'pose so. Still, I'm embarrassed sometimes. Do

you know you're the first person who's ever been to my house."

"Wow! I'm honored! Why me?"

"I just knew you wouldn't judge, because you're my friend."

Taylor's heart sank at Sara's trust in her, a trust she felt she didn't deserve. Then she plunged in. "Sara, I have a confession to make..."

* * *

It was time to clear the air. Taylor herself was getting along fine with both Sara and Vanessa, but Sara and Vanessa were still avoiding each other and had been for almost a month. So Taylor called a meeting of the three musketeers.

What she had neglected to tell Vanessa was that Sara would be there, and coincidentally Taylor had "forgotten" to tell Sara that Vanessa was also invited. Taylor didn't want them to come up with excuses for not getting together. She just hoped her plans for getting the threesome back together didn't backfire.

Taylor had everything prepared up in her bedroom. Snacks and beads were all set up. So when Vanessa arrived, Taylor took her straight upstairs and the two of them got started on their next projects. Christmas was fast approaching.

When the doorbell rang downstairs, Vanessa didn't appear to notice. Taylor knew what the doorbell meant, but she had asked her mom to bring Sara upstairs. When Taylor heard the footsteps on the stairway, she felt major butterflies doing flip-flops in her stomach. *Oh Lord, please help me say and do the right things, so we can heal the three musketeers.*

There was a knock on Taylor's door. Taylor sprang up and opened the door. Sara was just saying her usual "Hey, Taylor," when she stopped in mid-hey. She had seen Vanessa and Vanessa had seen her. When Taylor saw how uncomfortable both her friends were, she immediately regretted her decision to ambush them this way. Then she thought, *Too late now. God, it's in your hands.*

Taylor pulled Sara inside, and shut the door. Sara leaned up against the door, not relaxed enough to sit down.

Never before had these three girls been in the same room for more than three seconds in silence! This time, none of them spoke for over a minute.

Then Taylor took the initiative, and said, "Okay. I called this meeting, so I guess I should talk first." She looked around at her two best friends, took a deep breath, and said her piece. "I'm sorry if I've made you mad by not warning you that we'd all be here, but I've been so worried about our friendship. We have had such good times together, and I for one am not ready to dissolve the three musketeers. I don't know what's keeping you two apart, and I think we should talk about it."

More silence. Sara and Vanessa were still fidgeting and looking around, anywhere but toward each other.

Seeing that her friends were not ready to talk, Taylor pressed on. "Okay, I'll tell you what I know. I know that friends are important and that God wants us to build each other up. I also know that a while ago I had a misunderstanding with a friend because I jumped to a wrong conclusion. I thought Sara had dumped the three musketeers for Frannie. Then Sara explained that she and Frannie are friends, sure, but they were spending every second of the day together because of an important history project. So, Nessa, why can't we get back to where we were before this all happened? You know it was all a mistake, right?"

Vanessa nodded. "I understand about Frannie, yeah. But I'll tell you the truth. I've never felt right about Sara being one of us, Taylor."

Taylor's jaw dropped. "Pardon?!"

"You heard me, Tay," Vanessa insisted. "You've been my best friend since we were in diapers. I guess I'm jealous."

Sara couldn't contain herself any longer. "You're jealous? Of me? You with the swanky house and the private school and the parents with the fancy jobs and tons of money. You're jealous of me? That's a joke!" Vanessa had turned to face Sara now. "Yes, I am jealous of you, Sara. There's that church thing that you two share that I don't understand at all. Plus, I've always been able to pretend the Solomons were my other family, and I don't want to share them with anyone. You have your own family!"

Taylor had never heard Vanessa talk like this before. She always pretended to be so "together".

"I sure do! Seven kids, my mom trying to keep us all fed and clean, my dad hardly ever working. Yes, I have my own family!" Taylor heard that bitterness again.

"But, don't you see?" Vanessa continued. "That's one of the things I'm jealous about? I hear you talk about your folks and your brothers and sisters. Sometimes you're really ticked off with them, but underneath there's always such love. You all care about each other so much. And I'm green with envy. You have no idea how lonely it is in that big old house of ours after you guys leave, and I wait and wait for my folks to come home. Then when they do come home, they're so tired from work, or sometimes they're excited about work. What they're not excited about is seeing me." Vanessa was crying now. Sobs wracked her tiny shoulders. Taylor went over to try to hug her, but Vanessa didn't want to be hugged.

"I had no idea...," Sara said faintly. "And all I could think of was that big old house of yours and how beautiful it was and how much stuff you guys have. I never thought about your side of it at all. I'm so sorry." Sara moved toward Vanessa. She reached out her hand and gently touched Vanessa's arm. Then Vanessa's arms both reached out, and the three musketeers shared a warm hug.

When the tears had been shed and the eyes had been dried,

the three musketeers got back to their beads. As they were working, Sara came up with a great idea. "Nessa," she offered with a twinkle in her eye, "I'd love to lend you my sisters and brothers. I love them, but they're a bit much sometimes. Can I call you sometimes for help?"

"Great!" Vanessa laughed. "And if you ever need some peace and quiet, I have about a hundred empty rooms you can use."

"Sounds like a deal!" Sara agreed happily.

Taylor just watched her friends in amazement.

* * *

That night, the three musketeers shared dinner at the Solomon table. Jake had barbequed steaks, in spite of the snow flying outside on the patio. Julianna and Taylor had done inside duty, preparing salad, broccoli, and baked potatoes, and Sara and Vanessa had prepared a dessert with jelly and fruit and whipped cream. No one knew what it was, but it looked great!

When everyone was at the table, Jake said grace. "Lord, we thank you for your bounty, for the food you have provided for us – even the mystery dessert – and we thank you especially for the friendship between these three precious young women."

After the amens, Julianna added her agreement. "I'm so glad you guys have patched things up. I've been missing your faces around here!"

Everyone laughed and dug in, for a feast even Solomon would have enjoyed.

BIRTHDAYS
(Matthew 6: 34, Proverbs 12: 22)

Emma Solomon was playing her violin in a sunny alcove in the Solomons' living room when the telephone rang. She knew both the twins, Tim and Taylor, were home to answer it, so she tried desperately to ignore the shrill signal. She was working on a piece that she would play both in the Christmas show at school and as part of the pageant at church. Practice was not going well.

Emma was a very good musician, especially for her age. She would be ten on her next birthday, December 24. Emma had been looking forward to her birthday, and to Christmas; but lately she was dreading the approaching holiday because of the two upcoming concerts.

The school show was only a week away, on December 19; the pageant was the following Sunday, just before Christmas. Emma was going to play "What Child is This?" and she absolutely adored its kind of spooky melody. She had been working hard on it since the beginning of November though, and she was still having a very hard time with some parts of it. She really wanted to do well. Her three siblings were sports-crazy, but she preferred music; and she wanted her family to be proud of her.

"Emma Sue, it's for you," her thirteen-year-old sister Taylor chanted from the upstairs hall. "It's Angela."

"Oh no," Emma said to herself. Angela Pastorelli was her very best friend and her next door neighbor, but when you were on the phone with her you couldn't get off! She didn't want to hurt Angela's feelings, but she really had to practice. "Taylor, can you tell her I'm not here? I really need to work on this."

"No way!" Taylor called back. "Besides, she heard you playing when I picked up the phone. She thinks you need a break."

Emma carefully placed her violin on the sofa close to her music stand and went to the phone in the kitchen. "Hi, Ange!" she said, as cheerfully as she could manage.

"Hi, Em! How're ya doin'? I can hear you practicing all the way across here, you know, and you've been at it forever!"

"Yeah, I know," Emma agreed. "But I haven't done it right yet! I just can't get it! It's driving me crazy! But you know what they say: 'Practice makes perfect', right?"

"Right!" Angela teased. "But they also say, 'All work and no play makes Emma a boring best friend'–or something like that! Wanna come over for a while? I've got this amazing violet nail polish that you'll love. We could do our nails! And besides, I've got some great news!"

"News?" Now, Emma didn't know what to do. She should keep practicing, but she really wanted to know Angela's news. "Can you wait for about fifteen minutes? I just want to try one more time. Then I'll be over. I'll call you back if it's not okay with my folks."

Now, what could that be about? Emma wondered. She knew Angela sometimes over-dramatized things – it was part of why Emma liked her so much. Angela was what the adults called a "free spirit", whatever that was. It seemed to refer to her bubbly sense of fun and her wacky wardrobe, including a hat every single day. She had a great collection of hats – all shapes, colors, sizes, and styles.

But Emma had heard something in Angela's tone of voice that made Emma realize that her friend had some news that was really important, not just fun. That made it even more urgent to Emma than practicing for her two shows.

* * *

Three questions were on Emma's mind when, twenty minutes later, she rang the Pastorellis' doorbell: First, which hat would Angela be wearing? Second, what was Angela's news? And third, when would someone come to open the door? It was cold and snowy out there!

Emma finally heard Angela's footsteps thundering down the stairs. When the door opened, even Emma was stunned by the answer to question number one: Angela's hat today was shocking orange with a red brim and a purple pompom. Emma laughed. "Where did you get *that* one, Ange?" she asked, taking off her coat and wet shoes.

"My dad sent it to me from Venice Beach – that's in Los Angeles. I can show you the pictures he sent me, if you want. So, is this hat awesome or what?" Angela turned around to give her friend the full effect of all sides of her new headgear.

"What will you do to me if I say, 'Or what'?" Emma loved to tease her friend about her hats. Secretly, she adored every one of them and wished she had the nerve to wear them!

Emma laughed as she felt one of Angela's bony elbows jab her in the ribs. Then Angela grabbed her arm and dragged her up the stairs to her room. When they got there, she made a big show of checking in the hallway to see if her mom was there, or her little brother Bobby. Then she shut the door behind them.

"Okay, Ange, what's up? Why all the mystery?" Emma asked, as she flopped into one of Angela's multicolored beanbag chairs.

"You have to keep this a secret, Em," Angela whispered. "No one else knows – not even my mom. And she might not be glad to hear it, so I have to be careful when I tell her." She stopped talking – unusual for Angela – and just grinned.

Emma leaned toward her, anxious to hear the news. "What? What? Come on, Ange. You're killing me with suspense!"

"It's my dad," Angela was trying to whisper, but she was too excited to succeed. "He's coming for my birthday! For our birthdays, I should say." Angela had also been born December 24, but the year before Emma. Angela was turning eleven just before Christmas. "He sent me a note in the package with this cool hat, saying he'd be back here by Christmas and would come to see me. Isn't that too cool?"

Uh oh, Emma thought to herself, *here we go again*. A half-hearted "Wow" was all she could muster. She didn't want to destroy her buddy's excitement, but Angela's dad had made these promises before. Roberto Pastorelli had moved away from his family just after Bobby had been born seven years earlier. Since then he had promised to come back many times – but he had only actually visited a few times.

"Let me show you the note," said Angela, as she jumped off her bed and started rooting through the papers on her desk. "You have no idea how much I was hoping and praying this would happen. Imagine! My dad here for my birthday, and for Christmas too! We'll be a family again! Oh, here it is!" She handed the note to Emma with a flourish. Emma looked down at the piece of paper she now held in her hand. It was a napkin advertising 'Tony's Ribs'. The note scribbled on it said:

> *Dear A*
> *L.A. is fab! Sunny. Lots to do and see.*
> *Back in your area mid-December. See ya*
> *then. Love ya.*
> *Robo*

"Robo?" Emma read aloud.

"Yeah. You know my dad: he thinks titles like 'dad' take away from his individuality."

"But I thought you were supposed to call him 'Dome'."

"Not since he's letting his hair grow back in. Now it's Robo. I think it suits him, don't you?"

"S'pose so," Emma muttered. Emma tried to like Mr.

Pastorelli, but she didn't like what happened to Angela when she heard from him. It was all Angela could think about and talk about for days. Then something bad would happen, her dad would call with an excuse, and Angela would be mopey and sad for days after that. It wasn't fair!

"Are you sure he means to come *here*, Ange? I mean, it only says he'll be in the area. Knowing your dad, that could mean anywhere East of the Rockies, not necessarily Parkesville. And he doesn't say anything about your birthday or about Christmas. I hate to be the one who reminds you of this, but he forgot your birthday last year, remember?"

"I remember..." Angela was quiet for a moment. "But this is different. I just know it! You'll see. He'll be here."

"Well, I hope you're right, mon amie, but try not to count on it, okay?" Emma wanted to be more enthusiastic, but it was hard. There was an awkward pause in the conversation, as Emma tried to think of the right thing to say next, so she wouldn't hurt her friend's feelings. "Your dad is so funny. And he even brought *me* a present when he came by the last time! Taylor likes to put that rubber tarantula in the laundry basket now and again! My mom is not impressed!"

Angela grinned. "I'll just bet he'll bring me a California outfit to go with this hat! Or something even better!" she said.

"Well, I wonder what color his hair will be this time, now that he's growing it back in!" Emma teased.

"*If* he grows it back in...," Angela shot back.

Both the girls giggled. Once they got started, they could tell stories about Angela's dad all afternoon!

* * *

"Oh, Angela," Emma whined, "I just don't think I can even show up tonight for the school show! Dress rehearsal was a disaster! You were great, but I stunk!"

119

Emma and Angela were walking home from school the afternoon of December 19. They had both performed that afternoon in a dress rehearsal presented for the primary and junior classes at Col. G.P. Brady Public School. Angela had been a favorite with the younger children, in her role as Rudolf in the Drama Club's hilarious version of "Twas the Night Before Christmas". Emma, on the other hand, had made a few mistakes in her violin solo and the audience wouldn't sit still during her performance.

"Come on, Em, it wasn't that bad," Angela reassured her. "You can't expect a bunch of rugrats to enjoy classical music."

"'What Child is This?' isn't exactly classical music," Emma retorted. "It's a well-known Christmas carol."

"Well-known for us, maybe, Emma, but remember that most of the kids at Col. Brady don't know much about the real meaning of Christmas."

"Maybe so, but I still goofed up on the refrain – after all my practicing!"

Angela put an arm around Emma's shoulders. "Why don't we talk about something else; you know, take our minds off tonight. I'm nervous too, you know. Ms. Brown told us we should all just go home and 'forget it' for a while, remember. So what do you want to do?"

"I guess practicing is out, right? Let me think. Hey, I know: you never showed me those photos your dad sent from California. Do you want to look at them now?"

"Uh, yeah...cool idea," Angela agreed. But she didn't sound very enthusiastic.

"So, when is your dad coming?" Emma suddenly realized that her friend hadn't mentioned her dad all week. She guessed that it was all the Christmas activities that had distracted her.

Angela took a minute to reply. "I don't know yet. Uh..., he sent me a postcard. From Seattle, I think it was... Or Las Vegas... Or was it Toronto? I don't remember exactly, but he should be here any day now. I can't wait to see my birthday presents." Angela was staring at the ground ahead of her and dragging her boots through the snow on the sidewalk as she spoke.

It wasn't like Angela not to have details about her dad memorized and ready to put into every possible conversation. There was something Angela wasn't sharing, Emma just knew it. But she couldn't think about that now, with the school show threatening disaster that night. She knew her friend would tell her eventually.

"So, your place or mine?" Emma asked. "I think my mom made peanut butter chews today, plus there should still be some of those Christmas cookies you helped us decorate last week – unless Tim has polished them off already."

"Well, it's a cinch that there's nothing at my place! My mom is always too busy to bake. Let's go to your place!" A mischievous look crossed Angela's face, as she swung her book bag around and gave Emma such a whack on her behind that Emma suddenly found herself sitting in a snow bank. Laughing, Angela called out as she ran off, "What's keeping you? Last one to your place gets cookie crumbs!"

* * *

Emma needn't have worried: the school show was a huge success! Angela and the other drama kids were, once again, the hit of the show, but this time Emma was very pleased with her own performance. In fact, she knew it was the best she'd ever done.

Emma's parents and her siblings all agreed with her, amidst all the teasing. Tim couldn't resist saying, "Well, Sis, does this mean we don't have to wake up at 5 every morning to 'What Child is This?'" Taylor was a little more encouraging: "That was good, Emma Sue. I didn't feel a bit like nodding off."

Seven-year-old Peter, who had been fighting a cold, *did* nod off! Emma didn't mind; it was past his bedtime anyway!

Emma's parents, Jake and Julianna Solomon, were very proud of their young musical genius and told her so with wild applause after her performance, and with smiles and hugs at the end of the show.

"Now, I just have to get through the church concert on Sunday," Emma moaned, when they were in the van on the way home.

"Emma Solomon, you're going to give yourself an ulcer!" Julianna teased. "Do you know what Jesus said about worrying? In the Sermon on the Mount, he said, 'Do not worry about tomorrow, for tomorrow will worry about itself.' And here's my favorite part, especially in *this* family: 'Each day has enough trouble of its own.'" Julianna grinned at her children, who were sitting in the their regular seats in the rear of the van, boys in back, girls in front.. "You did a great job today, Emma, and you'll be even better on Sunday, especially with an audience of people who love that song as much as you do."

Emma smiled. Her mom always knew just what to say to make her feel better.

Then her dad quipped, "Besides, today has enough worries for us all. I don't know about you, but I'm not nearly finished my Christmas shopping – and there's also a birthday party to plan for two girls I know."

Emma smirked. "I wonder who," she said. "Oh hey! Do you know what present Angela is getting? Her dad is coming for Christmas!"

Jake and Julianna looked at each other. Emma's parents obviously knew something that she didn't, and their frowns also told her that she shouldn't say anything more about that particular topic. *Oh no*, Emma thought to herself. *Poor Angela. It's happening again.*

* * *

When Emma came home from school the next day, she could hear her mom talking to Teresa Pastorelli in the kitchen. Angela's mom must have stopped in on her way home from the Parkesville General Hospital where she was a nurse. Emma was starving, so she made her way toward the voices.

"But I told her he wasn't coming," Emma heard Mrs. Pastorelli say with a sigh. "He's changed his plans and has headed to a beach in Mexico for Christmas. I never know what to say to make Angela feel better. It's been so much harder on her than on Bobby. Bobby hardly remembers Roberto at all. But Angela loves Roberto so much, she just can't help hoping he'll change into the dad she wants him to be."

Emma knew it wasn't right to eavesdrop, but she was so shocked that she couldn't move from her place just outside the kitchen door. Mr. Pastorelli wasn't coming! Angela had lied to her! Her best friend had lied to her! Emma knew that Angela wouldn't lie to her unless ... Unless what? What excuse was there? What could she be thinking?!

Emma went up to her room to think about the conversation she had overheard. Obviously, there had been no postcard from Angela's dad, so why would Angela have said there was? Emma had actually begun to believe that Mr. Pastorelli was on his way home, because Angela had seemed so sure about it. Emma had been looking forward to seeing him again. And now, to find out it was all a lie. What a disappointment.

Then Emma realized how incredibly selfish she was being. Here she was feeling sorry for herself because Angela's dad was not coming to see *her*, all the while forgetting how crushed Angela must be. Angela's dad had let her down *again*.

Now, Emma was angry with herself for her selfishness, but even more so at Mr. Pastorelli. Where did he get off acting this way? Always making promises he didn't keep. He didn't seem to care at all about Angela and Bobby or about how much he hurt them. He didn't keep his word, but he always got away with it. It just wasn't fair! Emma picked up her violin and played, as loudly as she could, the first song that came into her mind: "Three Blind Mice", of all things.

Sometimes Emma wished she knew how to use a baseball bat!

* * *

Emma tried to talk to Angela the whole next day, but Angela avoided her, pretending to want to get all her homework done before Christmas holidays started. Angela could avoid her friend no longer, though, when the Pastorellis and Solomons joined up for brunch after church on Sunday, as they often did.

When they all got to the Chicken Delite, Emma slid in next to Angela on one of the benches. Emma couldn't help noticing that Angela had tried to move, but all the seats were already taken. Emma was still excited following the success of the church Christmas pageant, so she tried not to worry about it.

By the time they got their chicken fingers, though, Angela had still not said a single word to Emma. They had pretended to be having a good time, trying to join in the conversations all around them; but both girls were very uncomfortable.

When Angela excused herself to go to the washroom, Emma followed her.

"Why is it," they heard Tim muttering, "that girls always go to the washroom in pairs? I've always wondered." The girls could hear laughter from their table, as the door shut behind them in the empty institutional-pink Chicken Delite washroom.

Emma reached out for Angela's arm to stop her from hiding in one of the cubicles. "Okay, Angela, what's going on?" she wanted to know.

"What do you mean, 'What's going on?' Nothing's going on," Angela replied, defensively.

"It sure is," Emma insisted. "You're hiding something from me, and I want to know why."

"I'm not hiding anything. What makes you think that?"

"Well, for starters, you haven't said two words to me since we got here – not for days, in fact! You've been avoiding me, and I don't get it."

Angela was silent for a moment, until she couldn't hold in her feelings any longer. "And you will never get it, Emma Solomon, because you have the perfect father! You'll never understand how it feels to have a dad who doesn't care if you're alive! A dad who breaks every promise he ever makes. A dad who doesn't love you..." Tears streamed down Angela's face, and she didn't try to hold back her sobs.

"Oh Ange...," Emma whispered, as she put her arm around her friend's heaving shoulders.

When Angela's sobs were settling down, a teenager came in to use the mirror. The girls were glad of the distraction and became mesmerized as the girl reapplied layers of makeup, combed her hair three different ways, and adjusted her bell bottoms over her hips. This performance gave Angela time to take a deep breath, dry her tears, and pull herself together.

When the older girl finally left, Emma and Angela looked at each other and burst into the giggles. "Please tell me we're not going to be like that!" Emma said.

"Are you kidding?" Angela replied. "I just loved that orange eye shadow. And those pants were the best! Don't you think they'd look great with my Venice Beach hat?"

The mention of the Venice Beach hat suddenly brought the girls back to what they had been talking about before the teenager had come in. They looked at each other in silence. Then both of the girls started to talk at once.

"I'm so sorry...," Emma began.

"I didn't know what to do...," Angela started. "No, Emma, let me finish. I never got anything from my dad after my new hat and that little scrap of napkin. I kept rushing to the mailbox, but nothing came. Then he telephoned one night after Bobby and I were in bed and talked to my mom. Of course, he wouldn't be able to talk to me directly when he knew how disappointed I'd be. You'd think I'd learn, wouldn't you?"

"Well, I wish you'd told me," Emma said. "I can't change your dad, but maybe I can make you feel better about it all."

Angela thought for a moment before she could speak. "You know, Em, I think I was hoping that if I didn't say my dad wasn't coming that maybe he'd show up. Does that make sense?"

"A little..."

"And I felt stupid, falling for another of my dad's stories. I should know by now not to count on seeing him until he's standing on the doorstep. I was afraid you'd say, 'I told you so.'"

"I might have, at that! I did try to warn you not to get too excited," Emma said. "But I'm so sorry. I wish I could just share my dad with you, but I know it's not the same. And your dad does love you, you know."

"I suppose he does, in his way..." Angela tried to smile. "My mom keeps telling me that God is my Father and that he'll never let me down. I know that it's true, but sometimes I just want a great big Robo hug."

Emma gave her friend a great big Emma hug instead.

* * *

When Emma and Angela came back to the table arm in arm, everyone applauded. "We were about to send in a search party for you two," Jake Solomon joked.

126

THE WISDOM OF THE SOLOMONS

"So did you two patch it up?" Teresa Pastorelli asked her daughter. "We've all been worried about you."

"Yes, Mom," Angela replied. "It was all my fault. I lied to Emma about Dad not coming and I really hurt her feelings. I'll never do that again! I promise, Em."

Taylor happened to look over at her mother, who was deep in thought. "Uh oh, everybody, something tells me that my mom wants to tell us what her good buddy Solomon has to say, right, Mom?"

Julianna Solomon smiled. "You guessed it. Solomon has a lot to say about lying, but I can remember one very simple proverb: 'The Lord detests lying lips, but he delights in people who are truthful.' We've all seen today how a lie can come between even the best of buddies. Bad news, right?"

Everybody nodded, except Angela's little brother Bobby, who had slid under the table in search of a plastic snake that he'd just pulled out of the Chicken Delite treasure box.

The Solomons and the Pastorellis all went back to their various conversations and their desserts. They could hear Christmas carols playing in the background. Part of their celebration was for the birth of the Christ Child 2000 years ago; and part was for a young Solomon and her best friend who had learned the pain caused by lying lips, and the joy of forgiveness.